# Behavior Never Lies

by

## Richard Flint

*Learning The Eight Step Process*
*For Creating Consistency Between*
*What One Says and What One Does*

Published 2006
Copyright 2006

ISBN# 0-937851-33-7
Flint, Inc. Product #3012

*Printed in the United States of America.*
*For information write to*
*Flint, Inc.,*
*11835 Canon Blvd., Suite C-105,*
*Newport News, VA 23606-2570*
*or call 1-800-368-8255*

**www.RichardFlint.com**

Cover Design by Denise Smith

# DEDICATION

*This book is dedicated to Spencer Hayes whose presence in my life taught me the power to having a consistent presence.*

# TABLE OF CONTENTS

*BEHAVIOR NEVER LIES*

# Preface

*A Personal Message From Richard Flint:*

For years I have been a student of human behavior. I am always amazed at the mess a person can make with their life. One would think as intelligent as people are, they would see what they are doing and not leap over a ledge where they know they will get hurt. My challenge is I expect people to live with common sense. The truth is people don't lack common sense; they just choose not to use it. The result is a life they have to keep emotionally cleaning up. That takes so much time and energy. It can trap a person in a world of confusion. Each day a person only has two choices for that day of their life. They either choose to:

> • *feed their confusion*
> • *strengthen their clarity.*

If one really thinks about this, those are the only two choices a person has for a day of their life. Each day they choose one of these two as their pattern for living, make decisions based on their choice and implement behaviors to carry out their decision.

The funny, yet not so funny, part of this is their reaction to the mess they got into. They just can't believe this is happening to their life. They don't understand how this could be happening to them. They wonder what happened to create the mess they have gotten their life into. Their lack of holding self accountable for the mess their life is in becomes the foundation for their blame, excuses and justification for their life being the way it is.

That is the reason I wrote <u>Behavior Never Lies</u>. For

i

years I have listened to people explain, excuse, blame and justify the struggles they have in life. I have sat, listened, watched and thought, *don't they get it. One can explain, excuse, blame and justify all they want, BUT life is the result of the choices one has made and the behaviors they have implemented.* With each situation where people kept creating confusion I would continually keep coming back to three words, *Behavior Never Lies!*

The essence of any person is not what they say; *it is what they do.* Where there is disconnect between what is said and what is done, there is a contradiction. That contradiction creates confusion for the person and for those who are listening and accepting what is being said. Those contradictions will be demonstrated through a person's behavior.

The contradiction between what is said and what is done will cost one the trust of others. When a person makes a promise, and a statement of intent as a promise, and then, doesn't deliver people soon stop trusting them.

The contradiction between what is said and what is done will cost one the respect of others in and around their life. When people can't believe what one says, they soon stop listening because they don't trust the words being spoken, nor respect them as a person.

The contradiction between what is said and what is done weakens a person's presence. If the desired result of a life is to create a presence that has presence when they are not present, then the confusion between words and behavior will result in the weakening of one's presence. Having a presence that is present when one is not present is the greatest statement of respect any person can have.

This book is about helping people face their inconsistencies. It is about challenging the lack of connection between what is said and what is done. It is a practical guide to understanding how to create a common agenda between one's mind and their emotions. Without this common agenda there is constant internal conflict, which is demonstrated through one's behavior.

Behavior Never Lies offers the reader eight steps designed to balance their words with their behavior. The pages are filled with insights to guide a person beyond their confusion and on the right track to achieving consistency in their life. These pages will examine and challenge the design a person has chosen for their life. The book will confront the emotional entanglements that keep a person from having the consistency. The eight steps to creating balance will clarify what one must do to create the respect that allows them to have that presence that is present when they are not present. These eight steps are not a magical formula, but a pathway to connecting words with behavior. These eight steps are:

### Step 1: Believing In You

*Without a strong foundation of self belief a person will constantly be struggling with doubt, worry and a sense of uncertainty.*

### Step 2: Expanding Your Horizon

*When yesterday is what is creating your picture of today, you will find yourself repeating the things you have promised you wouldn't continue to do.*

### Step 3: Holding Yourself Accountable

*Until you can face your life with a sense of honesty, you will find yourself having to justify all those things you know you shouldn't have done or continue to do.*

**Step 4: Addressing Your Inconsistencies**
*Inconsistencies create the contradictions that keep you at war with yourself.*

**Step 5: Very Carefully Align Yourself With The Right People**
*The wrong people offer you a wrong direction; the right people take you in the right direction.*

**Step 6: Increase Your Awareness**
*The sharper your mental sight the easier it becomes to control your emotional reactions.*

**Step 7: Operating Your Life At A Manageable Pace**
*Either you are managing your life or your life is managing you.*

**Step 8: Refusing To Go Backward**
*As long as you are looking over your shoulder for answers, you are missing the lessons that are right beside you.*

These eight steps provide a picture frame in which a person can gain the clarity necessary to find the pathway through the confusion that is created when words and behavior are not in sync. The insights presented in these pages will give the reader the confidence to move forward with a sense of understanding and a belief that they can achieve the ultimate purpose for their life. It will clarify the fact *Behavior Never Lies!*

— Richard Flint

*BEHAVIOR NEVER LIES*

# The Purpose
## An Introduction

In 1980, before I started my speaking journey designed to help people understand how to improve their life, I had to gain a personal understanding of what I wanted to accomplish each time I walked out on stage, recorded a CD, filmed a video or wrote a book. I knew if I didn't understand why I was in their life, they would be confused by my presence. It was important that each person who experienced my presence be able to walk away feeling they had just been part of something that brought a new or renewed sense of value to their life.

I truly believe I can bring value to those who are serious about improving their life. My God given talent is the ability to help people see the pathway through the confusion that fills their life. Whether they want to admit it or not, confusion is a choice one makes which is acted out through behavior. If they are willing to face their behavior and redesign it, they can remove their confusion. If one chooses to live in confusion, their life will be filled with all the negative emotions confusion is designed to offer them.

I believe each day a person only has two choices about what that day will mean to their life. They choose to either feed the confusion in their life or strengthen their clarity. They will choose one of these and then implement behaviors to make their choice happen.

The challenge for me was taking what I understood to be my talents and blending them into a crusade where talent and insights came together to offer clarity. It took a lot of soul searching and mental processing to understand the result I wanted to offer those who choose to listen, to study or to watch my creations. Finally, I was able to put my crusade into a purpose statement.

My crusade is three fold. At the conclusion of my time with people I want them to:
- feel better about the purpose and direction of their life;
- be smarter and have insights they can implement to improve their life
- stand taller through their feelings of value and personal self worth.

When one can achieve these three things, they will understand the meaning of being free to live a life of personal discovery that will offer them calmness, clarity and confidence. This is the life that brings them the feeling of achievement.

**Feeling Better............**

Most people live a life trapped in their circle of sameness. It isn't they don't want to improve; they just want the improvement without having to change anything in their life. They know what they need to do, but their fear of doing it is greater than their desire to have something better. Anytime fear is greater than desire a person is trapped. When they are trapped, they design their life to repeat, not to improve and move forward.

To stay trapped in sameness one has to choose excuses and reasons as their justification for allowing their life to stand still. The tragedy is the mental and emotional damage it does to a person's life. It takes more energy to stay the same than it does to improve one's life. It takes more out of a person to emotionally remain the same than it does to implement the behaviors that will improve their life.

I've learned through the lives of people I have worked with that most of life's frustration, disappointments and depression is created by the inner battle between the circle of sameness and the desire to improve. Those who have understood and faced their behavior are today free from negative repetitive living and are moving forward with a clear purpose and a defined direction for their life.

When one feels better about their life, they are able to handle the worries, the doubts, and the uncertainties the circle of sameness throws at them. No, one is not free from their attacks, but are mentally and emotionally capable of not allowing the attacks to control their life.

Worry, doubt and uncertainty are all elements of negative fear. As long as negative fear grips one's life, they are a slave to the behaviors that keep them trapped in the Circle Of Sameness. Trapped in that circle, there is no way for a person to feel better about their life. In that Circle of Sameness, there is only constant mental and emotional drain.

A person can feel better, but feeling better is not about the issues one's life is handed. It is about the behaviors they bring to each issue. My desire, my crusade is to help each person feel better about SELF in order to really understand what there is for them to achieve with their life.

**Being Smarter............**

Have you ever known someone who had mastered the art of playing dumb? The statement is true – "God didn't create any dumb people." Playing dumb is a behavior one learns. Playing dumb becomes the way many avoid having to be accountable for their behavior. As long as those who have mastered the art of playing dumb are allowed to continue that behavior, they don't have to face what they are doing.

It is amazing how many of these people can manipulate others to feel sorry for them, make exceptions for them or validate their behavior by not holding them accountable. As long as they are protected, they have no reason to redesign any aspect of their life.

Besides, those who have mastered the art of playing dumb, there are also those who have chosen to waste their minds. Too many have given up being a student and learning. Many choose to become mental midgets and then, blame the issues of life as the reason they are stuck. When these people are not held accountable for their behavior, their behavior is validated. This feeds their justification and strengthens their screaming that "life isn't fair."

Truth is, life is always fair! What a person's life is, is exactly what they have designed it to be. One of the most powerful philosophies I have ever written is *you are perfectly designed to achieve what you are achieving.* Life is not about what is fair or unfair; it is all about what one is willing to do to improve their life. If they choose sameness as their life design, then they get the journey that goes with it, BUT if they choose growth and improvement as their life design, they get the journey that goes with that design. It is all about what ONE is willing to do. It is all about the behaviors ONE acts out each day.

Being smarter is about ONE being honest about SELF. It is about ONE removing the right to blame, to make excuses or to justify their actions. It is about ONE facing SELF and being honest about what THEY need to do to improve their life.

My crusade is about helping people develop their inner

strength to face self with honesty. It is about helping people arm themselves with insights that no longer allow them to give self permission to make excuses or use blame to justify the lies they have used to define their life. My desire is to help them become smarter by becoming a self-honest person.

**Being Taller............**

The #1 philosophy for my life is *why spend my energy being a carbon copy, when I am the original.* Until a person understands the concept of being an original, they will find themselves as an actor in someone else's play. That means each day they show up without the clarity to understand what a day of their life is handing them. It means each day ends with one wasting the greatest gift they have – time. It means each day they stand in the midst of the crowd of people who have given up their identity in order to allow someone else to define who they are, what they can achieve and where they are headed. These people become a sea of wasted humanity. As an actor in someone else's play, they give up their originality; they throw away their uniqueness; they live their life throwing away their talent and sinking deeper into a sinkhole that just keeps getting deeper and deeper.

Truth is that everyday one acts out, through behavior, what they really believe about who they are. One can say what they want with words, but who they really are is seen through their behavior. The foundation of all this is three little words – *behavior never lies!*

The essence of life is defined by behavior. Confusion is created when a person's stated words are contradicted by their behavior. Reality is behavior cannot lie. Behavior is always truth. Over the years, I have found this to be the one statement

I say that makes most people uncomfortable. They don't like hearing those three words. They don't like having those three words become the test of their life.

When words and behavior contradict each other, there can be no improvement. The contradiction creates confusion and confusion makes improvement impossible. That means as much as one talks about wanting to improve their life, until the contradiction is cleared they are trapped in a life that is based on a pattern of inconsistency.

When one's words and behavior are working together, they are unlimited in what they can achieve. That means they stand taller in their personal trust. That means one stands taller in their personal confidence. That means a person stands taller in the eyes of other people. When their presence has strength through behavior, they have a presence that is present even when they are not present. That is the definition of personal power.

Trust and confidence work hand in hand to strengthen one from the inside out. Trust is their inner belief in self and confidence is the outer demonstration of self-trust through behavior. My crusade is to help people stand taller in their personal trust and confidence.

**The Truth About Accountability............**

When I started my crusade to help people be better, smarter and stand taller, I just knew I was in the right place with the right message for the masses. I just knew when I arrived people would be waiting with open arms to hear my message, implement my insights and move forward with a life that offered them happiness, fulfillment and freedom. I just knew it was going to happen. How naïve I was!

It didn't take long to realize most people want to stay the same; most people find it easier to blame; most people have a reason why their life isn't; most people would rather spend their time justifying their lack of life, rather than facing their life with personal honesty and being willing to challenge their behavior in order to see what they can really become.

Society has made this okay. Study most business environments and you will see that rather than leadership challenging people to be better, to be smarter, to stand taller they have lowered the standards and made average their definition of good. Then, they wonder why the public has lost so much faith and trust in their ability to deliver quality. They don't want to face the fact that *average people can only deliver average results*. BUT, that is easier than stepping up as leaders that are requiring people to be accountable for their behavior. The result has been and continues to be a business environment that continues to preach customer care and deliver customer frustrations and disappointment.

Study the family and you will see most families unwilling to teach their children accountability or responsibility. Rather than teaching the principles of accountability and responsibility, they have jumped onto the bandwagon of blaming everything, but their lack of parenting, for the problems their children are facing. The result is a child unprepared to handle life. They have not had to be responsible as a child, so why should they be responsible as an adult. They have been sheltered and protected from the truth about their behavior, so they walk out unwilling to be responsible or accountable for who they are, what they have done or what they aren't doing. As an adult, their life becomes a continuation of their life as a child. If one has not had to be accountable as a child, do you think their adult life will automatically overcome that lack of accountability?

Even government lives in denial when it comes to accountability. Rather than facing the issues created by irresponsible behavior, they would rather throw money at people. If a person is taught they will be paid for doing wrong, what do you think they are going to do? How much of our government's spending is done so that politicians don't have to face the real issues? I am not opposed to welfare, but I am against handing people money when they are capable of working. As long as government refuses to make people accountable for their behavior, people will remain in their Circle of Destructive Sameness.

To many of those who have been elected to provide direction have given control of their voice to those who throw the most money at them. Their vote is for sale to those who can line their coffers with money or to the political pressure that says, "Stand the line" even when the line is not in the best interest of the people they are representing.

What happens to a society when greed becomes more important than ethical presence? What happens when the system of accountability has been weakened by an unwillingness to stand taller and stand true to principles that will make all accountable for their behavior? After all, *behavior never lies.*

## THE CHALLENGE BEHAVIOR NEVER LIES PRESENTS
During a radio interview about my book, **Breaking Free**, Mike, the show host, asked if I would stay on for a couple of minutes at the conclusion of the interview. When the

interview was over and the show had gone to commercial, he said, "Boy, I would not want your job."

His words took me by surprise and I responded with, "Why?"

"Richard," he said in a very serious tone. "I bet I am no different than other people who listen to you. I found myself agreeing with you, but at the same time not wanting to hear what you were saying. There is so much truth to what you say that it is frightening. I would bet the majority of people who listen to you like what you say, but hate listening to it. That has to make it very difficult for you."

"Mike, I wrestled with that when I started this crusade of helping people understand what they have to do to remove their confusion and reach the ultimate aspect of living. I knew from the beginning the masses would not accept me. I had to reach a mental place where that was okay. I know many who listen, watch or read what I have created are not going to enjoy the frankness and honesty of my approach. That's okay. My role is not to convince them, but to expose them to the truth about their life and their behavior. I can't, nor do I want to be responsible for what they do with it. That is their choice, and they will choose to either accept and implement or reject and justify."

"Doesn't that bother you?"

"In the beginning it did, but then, I realized I couldn't change the world. But I could have an affect on people who want to improve and are willing to face their life with honesty. That is all I want to do. I want to find the few who are ready and willing to take an honest look at their behavior and move beyond the world of excuses, reasons and justifications. Those are the people I want to challenge with insights and lessons that go beyond where others have stopped. One can't see beyond the limitations they have created for their life and those limitations are self-imposed. One is not limited by situations; situations are the test to see how much they understand about who they are. The test will expose how much they are willing to spend mentally and emotionally to achieve their stated dream. The tragedy is too many spend their life living a lie of words that is exposed by their behavior."

There was a pause and then this question stated in a very serious tone. "I've got to ask you. When you say you want to have an affect on those who want to take an honest look at their life, how many do you think that is?"

"Mike, it is 1%!"

"Only 1%? Are you serious?"

"Yes! Only 1% of people want to improve their life. The rest find it much easier to live in their world of denial. That world is designed around reasons, excuses and blame, which are all used to justify where their life isn't and why their life is filled with so many problems. The reality is it is their choice to either stay there or get out of the ugly trap they have made for themselves."

I refer to my conversation with Mike because it is very real to what you will experience in the pages of **Behavior Never Lies**.

There are no games played in the pages of this book. Life is not viewed from fantasyland; it is about real world, real experiences and sometimes tough to face situations. People, who are seeking to avoid facing their life with honesty, are going to be challenged by the pages of this book. In their world they write the rules and decide who gets to play and who doesn't. They only keep people around who support their games. Those who challenge their behavior are tossed aside with criticism and anger.

The insights contained in these pages will challenge opinions many have called beliefs. Many fail to understand a "belief" that can't be challenged is simply an opinion. So much of life's confusion is the result of wrong thoughts that have been made okay because no one challenged the behavior. The result is a life out of sync and guided by the confusion that results from the wrong behavior.

Some will find times when they just want to stop reading this book. It will not be because of the content; it will be because the content has connected to an area of their life they are either not prepared to face or don't want to deal with. What do most do when they disagree with something? They shut down and emotionally disappear from the conversation. Information one doesn't agree with should strengthen them. If a person can hear with their ears and their eyes and not run, they gain insights that strengthen their understanding of who they are and the purpose of their life.

This book is about being better, being smarter and standing taller in life. The stronger a person is internally the clearer their life becomes.

Read this book with an open mind and it will challenge and inspire you to improve your total life. I want you to be free to live the life God intended you to have. I want you to fully understand the power of those three little words, *Behavior Never Lies!*

*BEHAVIOR NEVER LIES*

Chapter 1

# The Misconceptions About Success

*Success is the feeling that goes with you being in control of your life.*

I asked Alex, "What do you want for your life?"

He looked at me with this expression of confusion on his face. "I want to be successful."

"What does that mean?"

"You know!"

"No, I don't. When you say you want to be successful, what does that mean to you?

"I want to have money, a nice house and all the things that go with being successful. I don't want my family to have to struggle; I want my kids to be able to go the finest schools. When I say I want to be successful, I want it all!"

I've had that same conversation with thousands of people and their answer doesn't vary much. They each see success as "having it all."

I was standing in Ted's kitchen studying the picture of the house taped to his refrigerator door. He walked over, looked at the picture and said with a grin on his face, "That's my dream house. When I have that house, I will have it made. That is when I will know I have achieved success."

I turned to him and asked a very simple question, "Ted, how are you going to get that house?"

The puzzled look on his face told me he hadn't figured that out yet. "I'm going to work hard, save the money and buy it."

"How long do you think it will take you?"

"At the rate I am going right now an eternity. I stand here everyday and look at it and know it is possible. I just don't have the plan in place to make it happen."

"Then, let me ask you a question. Does the picture of that house ever create frustration for you? You stand here, look at the house, and tell yourself you want it, but don't have a clue to how you are going to get that house. Does that ever frustrate you?"

"Yes! In fact lately it has happened more than ever before. Lately, I have been questioning whether I can ever get there. The energy that picture has created in the past has become weaker. The other day I almost took it down. I didn't, because I really want that house. It is a definition of success for me."

The world is filled with the Ted's; it is filled with people who have a picture of what they want, but no idea of how to get there. The result is a life that reaches into the darkness hoping to find a light switch that will give them what they want. They don't seem to understand it is not about finding the light switch! It is about preparing to enter the room. The light switch without the right preparation will only shed more light on the confusion that exist, not help a person find the door that takes them beyond their world of confusion.

I wish obtaining success was as easy as putting a picture on the refrigerator, looking at it and having it appear. If success were that simple, everyone would achieve it. Reality is, it is a process most are not willing to risk their life to have.

Everyone wants to be successful. Listen to people talk and listen to how much of their conversation is about what they want for their future. The challenge is most don't understand what achieving success means. As long as success is defined as "things," it will be an arena of confusion and frustration for most people. As long as people "wish," rather than dream, the pictures they have will remain undeveloped film.

For years I have listened to the great motivational gurus tell people, "If you believe you can, you can do it." They stand on stage and tell people, "No matter what is happening in your life tell yourself you are great and move on."

I am challenged by their teachings, because I know the teaching is hype, not reality. No matter how it is stated *a lie is a lie.*

I don't believe in the old adage, "What the mind can conceive the mind can achieve." As good as that might sound, the statement is not truth. I watch people everyday pump themselves up with positive mental attitude, walk out and fall flat on their face. Many would say, "That wasn't really believing in yourself." That is correct; that is using words to convince self of something one doesn't believe. That means the energy is good until one runs into a wall they can't see over. What happens to those who have convince self with the words that they can, but internally really don't believe what they have said? The first time they hit a wall they can't see through or over 99% will either sit down and blame or walk away by justifying.

I have spoken for several Multi-Level-Marketing groups. I love the possibility they offer people. Many have stepped in, stepped up and achieved more than they ever thought they could. Reality is these people are the exception, rather than the rule. The majority of the people, who get involved step in with great excitement, come face to face with their demons of fear and doubt, hit a wall and justify walking away.

Did these people want to be successful? YES! Did they enter thinking that just maybe this was their exit out of their Circle of Sameness? YES! Do most of these people not achieve what they set out to achieve? YES! Why?

I believe it is the result of an unrealistic definition of success! They are taught to "reach for," not prepare for. It is in that difference that their demise is created.

They are armed with excitement, not enthusiasm. The difference between the two is extremely important. When excitement doesn't mature into enthusiasm, there will be an emotional crash that leaves the person in a world of self-doubt.

What most people fail to realize is excitement is based on a possibility. That possibility is good to get one started, but cannot sustain the journey. When the obstacles appear, when the doubts creep in, when there are not the results they were counting on, the excitement dies and replaced by disappointment. That disappointment creates an emotional pit they fall into.

There is no value in excitement if it doesn't mature into enthusiasm. Excitement must be viewed as a starting point, not the journey. Why? Because excitement is emotionally based. It is driven by an emotional surge that has to constantly be replenished with positive results. If the well of excitement is not constantly replenished, it will dry up and leave a person in a wasteland filled with negative questions that create a larger world of self-doubt.

Enthusiasm is based in opportunity. When one is living with excitement, their emotions are controlling the journey. If the journey doesn't happen, the emotions grow and take over their definition of what is happening. The stronger the emotions, the more challenging it becomes to focus. When the focus is gone and one is left standing in the wasteland, they are emotionally trapped.

Enthusiasm is governed by opportunity. Opportunity is imagination based. When one's imagination is wide open and they can see beyond the moment they are standing in, there is the consistency of energy. When one's imagination is stronger than their emotions, they have motivation. Motivation is emotionally based, but imagination driven. When there is no imagination, one will live with momentary belief, which can rise and fall with their definition of what is happening.

I have spent years working with families. Do most people who get married want to live happily every after? YES! Do most feel they have found their soul mate? YES! Will many of these be part of a relationship that ends in divorce? YES! Is this what they wanted? NO! What happened?

I believe most of them had an unrealistic definition of what is involved in having a successful marriage. They enter "searching for, "not prepared" for learning to blend their personal uniqueness into behaviors that each can accept. Will the lack of acceptable behavior create conflict? Yes! If that conflict is not talked about, will it create a wall of silence that will strengthen their disappointment? Yes! Will that disappointment over a period of time create a form of separation between them? Yes!

Successful marriages are not about expecting people to become what one thinks they should become. It is about accepting the uniqueness of each and working to blend personalities. That requires listening to the person's behavior to learn whom they see themselves as.

I have spent years researching talented people who were driven by the desire to succeed. Do they have the inner hunger to succeed? YES! Do they have goals? YES! Will most of these talented people achieve the success they had planned for their life? NO! What happened?

I believe most of them had an unrealistic understanding of success. They have been programmed with unrealistic thoughts. They have been told they can't make it without goals, so they write goals and still don't make it. They have been told they need to work hard, so they work hard and still don't make it. They have been told they need to listen to tapes and CDs and read books, so they listen and read and still don't make it. They have been told they need to go to programs, so they spend a lot of money for programs and still don't make it.

I sat with a gentleman in Orlando who told me he had spent over $50,000 to attend educational programs and over $30,000 in buying educational materials. I watched the anger in his face as he talked about being trapped in the same Circle of Sameness he had been fighting for twenty years to get out of. As much as he thought he was doing what he needed to do to break free, he was still trapped in the same self-destructive circle. The more we talked the clearer it became to him that he had the material, but not the behavior to make it work. It was challenging for him to admit that, but behavior never lies.

Then, someone says, "The problem was they weren't really committed." These people I have researched were committed to achieving success, the truth was they didn't have a realistic understanding of success.

As long as people are programmed to stare at things and are not taught the real meaning of success, they are going to start journeys filled with excitement and end up sitting by the side of the road worn out from trying. The end result one desires doesn't guarantee they can get there. Success is not about what one wants; it is about the price they are willing to pay to obtain it and the behavior they implement as they make the journey.

**Understanding Success............**

Walk through the Self Development or Business section

of any bookstore and study the number of books that have been written on teaching people about success. Pick up most of the books and skim through them and there is page after page of information about achieving success. They basically all teach the same message. What will not be found is much information to help one understand what success is. Most talk about the results a person can achieve, not the journey success demands. My conclusion is results mean nothing if a person doesn't understand the journey to getting there. A journey without a map will only get one lost.

Others will talk about a process for obtaining success. Yet, when one reads what they are saying it is all the elementary principles that people have used for years that continue to frustrate people trying to make sense out of the process.

If a person was to lay all the material that has been written, filmed or recorded about success aside and really examined the concept of success, they would understand that success actually only has two ingredients – *knowledge and behavior.*

That's it! Two ingredients – knowledge and behavior. Armed with just these two one can understand the place of all the other ingredients that have been talked about for years. Without the understanding of the power and place of these two ingredients, one will face a world that steals their desire, leaves them unprepared, without the ability to focus, lacking discipline and ending each day wondering what is going to have to be done to get there. Reality is that what they are staring at is an illusion, not a journey.

I was talking to a gentleman about success only being about these two ingredients when he interrupted me and said,

"It can't be that simple! It has to be more than that."

Reality is achieving success is not difficult if one understands the structure they must have in place. Nothing in life is really complex until one denies the "right way" and starts fighting for the "wrong way" of doing anything.

When a person has the correct knowledge and applies that knowledge with the right behavior, there is very little that can stop them. When one has the correct knowledge and the right behavior they live in a world driven by calmness, clarity and confidence. With these three as their inner strength, they are free to soar beyond those who are limited by their lack of knowledge and behavior.

It is important to understand knowledge and behavior don't work independently of each other. It is not about either/or. They must both be in place and working together with a common mission based on a realistic agenda.

I have met many who have the knowledge, but lack the behavior and watched them remain trapped in their Circle of Sameness. I have also watched people who understood the correct behavior, but didn't have the knowledge to sustain the behavior. The result was the journey being short lived.

## Knowledge Without Behavior............

Dean is as intelligent as anyone a person will ever meet, but he is lazy. Sit and talk to him and he can wear a person out with what he wants to do with his life. He can walk one through what needs to be done, talk about how he intends on doing it, but he doesn't have the behavior to make it happen.

He was introduced to me by his wife who was fed up

with listening to him talk and then, not act. "Richard, I have had enough of this. For ten years he as talked about what he is going to do. For ten years he has lied to himself and others. When you made the statement tonight *Behavior Never Lies*, I reached over and punched him. He knew exactly what the punch meant."

She paused, looked at him with pain in her eyes and continued. "It is not that he can't do what he keeps talking about doing. He can. He is very talented, but he just won't get up off his butt and do it!"

I looked at Dean and asked, "Is that a fair assessment of your life?"

The sheepish look on his face told me the answer. "Yea, she's right. I know what I want; I know what it will take to do it, but I just can't get my mouth and my body on the same track."

Behavior Never Lies!

Ruth came to me after a presentation I did for the Virginia Association of Realtors. "You nailed me! I felt like I was the only one in the audience. When you said those three words, *Behavior Never Lies*, I knew you were talking to me."

She paused, took a Kleenex from her purse, wiped her eyes and continued. "Richard, I have been in Real Estate for sixteen years. I have been to the top of the sales chart. I was #1 in my office for years. Today, I am struggling. I have trouble getting out of bed in the morning. When I look at the things I know I need to be doing, I can justify not doing them. I have slipped into a world of good intentions."

Again, she paused to gather her emotions. "I have become a master of reasons. I have a reason for everything that doesn't get done. You really slapped me today. I sat there and had to admit I have been lying to myself. I know what I need to do. I have the knowledge. What I don't have is the behavior. Somewhere along the way I have given myself permission to lie. I will tell you that stops right here, right now! Thank you for waking me up to the truth I didn't want to hear."

Behavior Never Lies!

David and Judy approached me at the conclusion of my presentation at the Ohio Real Estate Investor Conference. I heard them coming. David was muttering to himself and Judy was crying.

"I don't know whether to hug you or punch you," were his opening words to me. "I needed to hear what you were saying, but I sure didn't want to hear it. When you said in your opening remarks that you were going to hit us with an honesty most of us would not like, I thought you were just joking. You weren't! I sat there listening and three or four times wanted to get up and leave. When you said those three words, *Behavior Never Lies*, I just died inside. You are looking at a person who has been lying to himself for many years. I knew it, but didn't want to admit it."

Judy walked over and took his hand. David took a deep breath and said, "In the past ten years I have spent thousands of dollars in courses and materials telling myself these were going to make me successful. I justified buying them under the pretense of needing more knowledge. Oh, don't get me wrong. I have listened to all of them at least once, but have never taken what I heard and translated it into action. You are so right when you say, *Behavior Never Lies*. It is hard for me to stand here and without getting emotional. I am guilty!"

Behavior Never Lies!

I was speaking for a Network Marketing Group in Chicago when I met the Miller's. Here was a dynamic young couple that had gotten into Network Marketing as a way to get Mike out of a job he didn't enjoy. They had examined several Multi Level Marketing concepts and felt this one was right for them. For three years they had faithfully attended every function, listened to every speaker and built a resource library second to none, BUT had not really done anything with their business.

As we sat down to talk, I could feel the emotions that were running through both of them. They were holding hands so tightly you could see their hands turning white.

"Relax," I said. "Let's just talk for a few minutes.

Mike looked at Alicia for a second and then said to me in an emotionally filled voice. "Thank you for being true to your words of not playing games. I really didn't believe you when you told us you were going to walk inside us and make us very uncomfortable. You were true to your word, but the truth is not easy to listen to. When you said those three words, *Behavior Never Lies*, we both knew you were talking to us."

He paused, looked at Alicia and continued. "Richard, we have been in the Network Marketing business for three years. We have never missed a major function. We have come and acted like we were people who were talking the walk and walking the talk. In reality our presence was a lie. We really do want to succeed in this business. Our Upline are two of the finest people we have ever met and they have been so kind to us. There is nothing they wouldn't do for us. We have also lied to them."

He paused again to regain his emotional presence. "This is a tough thing to say, but we have spent the last three years lying to ourselves about what we were doing. We know how to do this business. We have listened to really successful people speak; we have listened to great speakers share with us; we have the knowledge. What we don't have is the behavior. That is the piece of the puzzle that has been missing. *Behavior Never Lies!* Those words are now a permanent part of my life."

He looked at his wife, took her hand and with tears in his eyes said, "I am so sorry my behavior has made it so challenging for us to succeed. You have my word that I will strive to not contradict myself again. If you catch me, just look at me and tell me those three words, *Behavior Never Lies.*"

If one has the knowledge and not the behavior, they will end up stuck and having to justify what is not happening in their life. Success demands that knowledge and behavior work together. They are not independent of each other.

**Behavior Without The Knowledge.............**

I have also seen people who had the behavior, but lacked the knowledge. They thought if they just worked real hard they could make it through. The reality is behavior can only take one so far. If a person doesn't have the knowledge to go along with the energy, they will soon find themselves standing at a crossroad where their lack of knowledge will not allow their mind to show them the right direction. At that point anything they do will be a guess. At that point no matter how hard they work they will end up going in circles. Those circles will wear on their behavior and the wearing will wear them down and out.

Eddie was one interesting person. I met him on the golf course at Madison Green where I live. Jimmy, the starter, asked me if I would mind him joining me. I said, "No, that will be okay."

Jimmy leaned in, took my arm and said, "He is really an interesting person. I think you are going to have fun."

Little did I know how true his words were. Eddie was "Mr. Personality." He was a distributor for a line of automotive products. He was smooth, fast-talking and always quick with a joke and never met a stranger. Once he found out what I did, it didn't take him long to start telling me his life story. He was an orphan who learned at an early age to take care of himself. His parents turned him away when he was ten. His dad was an alcoholic and he told me he couldn't remember a time when he saw him sober. His words were, "He was one mean person. When he was drunk, he came looking for a punching bag. It was always me or my mother. Many times I would get between them and took the beating so he wouldn't hurt my mother. I really hated him!"

His mother worked three jobs to earn money to keep the family from going under. "She was a saint," were his words about her. "She had so much strength, but the weight of having to take care of the family was too much for her. It broke her mentally, emotionally and physically. It was so tough watching her break apart. There are times I still find myself crying when I think about her."

When he was ten, his parents took him to see his aunt. His parents told him he was going to be there a few days. That was okay, but the few days turned into a long nightmare. His parents never came back and when his Aunt died, he was left on his own.

We were sitting in the clubhouse after our round of golf when the majority of his life was unfolded to me. He didn't ask if I had time to listen. I was the set of ears he needed to empty his emotional vault.

"If I inherited one thing from my dad, it was the gift of gab. I have always been a talker. I learned early on to use my personality to get me through situations. There weren't many things I couldn't bluff my way through."

He paused, got that little kid look on his face and said in a laughing tone. "Hell, I don't know anything. I just wear people down with my gab."

I could see that behind that laughing tone was a lot of hurt and pain. I didn't push him to talk about anything, but what he wanted to talk about. We sat there for almost three hours with him sharing pieces of his life.

Finally, he looked at his watch and said with a laugh "Wow! I have really bent your ear. I am sorry. I don't know why I have told you all this."

He stopped, stared out of the window for a minute and turned back to me with a very serious look on his face. "Richard, do you think you could help me?"

"Where do you think you need help?"

"I guess you can tell that I am a lot of hot air. I am not married, but would like to be. I seem to destroy every relationship I get. I have a business, but I don't know how to run it. I burn so many bridges with customers. I win them with my personality, but lose them with my lack of understanding. Do you think you could help me define a growth plan for my life that would make me more than just a personality who blows a lot of smoke? I want more out of life than what I have. I want to be more than what I have been. I want to learn how to be more than Mr. Personality."

Eddie was a lot smarter than many who are like him. He understood that personality could only take a person so far. When the tests of life come, it is not simply about knowledge or behavior; it is about the two working together. If one has the behavior, but not the knowledge, they are limited to how much they can achieve with their life.

It is not either/or. It is knowledge and behavior working together to define life.

Gary and Regina came to me when they were at their wits end with Matt, their 15 year old son. I could see their stress before they ever started talking.

"Richard," Gary said with a mixture of anger and hurt. "We are at our wits end with him. We don't know what to do. We recently found out that he isn't going to school. He leaves the house each morning and spends the day with a group of kids that has also dropped out. He lies to us all the time. We don't trust him and we can't believe what he tells us. We just don't know what to do. Would you visit with him, please?"

When Matt arrived, his demeanor said he didn't want to be there. He came into my office, plopped down in a chair and just stared out the window.

"Matt, do you know why you are here?"

"Because my mom and dad are punishing me."

"I don't think it is because they are punishing you. It is because they are really concerned about you."

"Why? There is nothing for them to be concerned about."

"What about the lying you have been doing?"

"I only do that because they can't handle the truth. They don't really want to hear how I feel. When I have tried to talk to them, they just fly off the handle. They are the ones who are lying."

"What about your dropping out of school?"

"School is boring. I don't need that crap."

"You don't think you need to get an education?"

"NO! School is over-rated. My friends didn't finish school and they are doing okay. What's the big deal about graduating? I can get a job without finishing school."

"You don't think not having a high school education will hurt you in the future?"

"I don't know, nor do I care. I just want to live my life and do what I want to do. If my parents don't like it, I will move out. I can get by and I can take care of myself."

That conversation happened over five years ago. Matt did move out and for a long time dropped off the planet. It drove Gary and Regina crazy. They didn't know where he was and even though they spent a lot of money searching for him, they couldn't find him. When Matt was 25, he called them and wanted to know if he could come home. They were surprised, thankful, frightened and nervous all at the same time. They didn't know what to expect, but told him to come home.

Regina, Gary and I spent time talking about how they should approach his homecoming. We talked about not being judgmental or being too hard on him. We decided they needed to let this be his conversation. They needed to listen and see what Matt had to say.

It was especially challenging for Regina. She wanted to pretend that nothing had happened and just welcome him back with open arms. It took a lot of talking for her to understand that couldn't happen. It took a lot of thinking through to face the fact that he had made the choice to leave, and they needed to understand why now he wanted to come back.

They were all a nervous wreck. When Matt left he was about 5"6" and weighed about 120 pounds. Now, he was 6'1" and weighed about 210. He didn't know how to approach his mom and dad. When the four of us later talked, he told me how scared he was.

"I know what I did was wrong, but at that time in my life I didn't like me, nor did I like them. I saw them as two people who wanted to put me in a prison and I wasn't going to let them do that. I can't believe how stupid I was."

I have this burning picture in my mind of him sitting between his parents, taking their hand, looking at them with tears coming down his face and saying "I am so sorry for all the hurt I caused you. I know my behavior was wrong, but I didn't know what to do, so I just ran away."

Matt went back to school, got his GED and today is a senior in college. I remember him telling me, "You know I hated you, don't you?"

"Yes, Matt. I knew I wasn't one of your favorite people."

"I thought you were taking up for my mom and dad. I now know you were really interested in me. There were many nights when your words would pound in my head. I would try to turn them off, but they were just too loud. You know – when you don't know what you don't know, you can really behave in some stupid ways."

It is not either/or. It is knowledge and behavior working together to define one's life.

Without knowledge a person is limited. They are forced to move in circles that keep bringing them back to the same roadblocks they have been wrestling with for some time. Knowledge is more than putting self in a learning situation. Each day as I stand on platform and present my research, it is so easy to pick out those who are there to gather insights they can implement into their life. The tragedy is these are the minority.

Constantly I am asked, "How many people do you think ever use the information you give them?" My answer is always the same – 1%! Most people are there looking for the quick fix. They want the instant answer they can use to solve all their problems without facing any of their issues. That doesn't work. There are no instant answers; there is only a process that takes time, commitment, discipline, patience and a strong desire to improve a person's life.

Knowledge is only power when one implements it and allows it to challenge their behavior. Knowledge that doesn't challenge is only information. Information creates stacks of stuff one plans on getting to some day. That "some day" is the tomorrow that never looks any different than today.

The implementing of knowledge is always visible through behavior. The visual part of learning is the redesigning of behavior.

I wish people could meet Matt. Matt is a very talented young man with a great desire for growth that for years was stifled because of his behavior. Oh, he lived with good intentions; he worked hard; he had goals; he even believed that someday he would achieve what he talked about.

I met Matt and Linda at a Robyn Thompson Real Estate Investment Boot camp where I was speaking. Robyn had told me about them and I was eager to get to know them.

We've heard it said that opposites attract. Well, there was no better illustration than Matt and Linda. They were more than opposites; at times they didn't even live on the same planet. Matt's behavior would drive Linda up the wall. She would challenge, push, prod and confront Matt, but Matt was living in his own world of self-denial. He knew he needed to improve his life, BUT each time he got close something would happen that would send him reeling backwards.

It took me four months of working with Matt's self-beliefs before he could begin to see himself from the inside out. It took him being willing to learn about his fears, being willing to face those fears and challenge the "Old" Matt who had control of his life. The turning point was Matt's willingness to gather knowledge that challenged his personal behavior.

Up to this point Matt had been concentrating on information designed to improve his business life. He listened, knew what he needed to do, but never quite got it done. That really frustrated him and upset Linda. She saw a Matt he couldn't see.

I designed a personal learning journey for Matt where he gathered insights about his behavior. I gave him two sets of audiotapes I had developed –"The Freedom To Soar" and "Getting Beyond Life's Negative Tapes." Those two CD packs challenged every lie Matt had been living. They opened him to the in-depth meaning of Behavior Never Lies.

He grew to understand the war between the "Old You" and the "New You" that is fought each day. He was awakened to the power the "Old" Matt had and how that power was demonstrated through his behavior.

Matt put it this way. "You didn't tell me anything I didn't know. You just made me face what I was doing. My life was filled with words that were contradicted by my behavior. No wonder my life was so confused. No wonder Linda struggled with me so much. I was a walking contradiction. My words were a lie that was proven by my behavior."

If one could meet Matt today, he is not the same person. He fought the battle between the "Old" and "New" Matt and "New" Matt won! He has created a pace he can manage, a plan his behavior doesn't contradict and a life that is filled with a continual gathering of knowledge. He is part of the 1%.

Success is not simply a plan. Yes, everyone needs a plan, but it is so much more. Success is not just about writing goals. Yes, one needs them to provide them with victories to gather energy from. Success is not simply about working hard. Yes, a person needs to work smart to reach their desired results.

Success is so much bigger than this. It is about gathering knowledge so one is not limited from a lack of insights. It is about taking the knowledge one gathers and applying it to their behavior. When knowledge and behavior come together on a growth journey, there is no stopping a person.

The essence of who one is, is defined by their behavior. Listen to what is being said and see if the words are supported or contradicted by one's behavior. A person's success will not be dictated by their words. One can have the greatest of intentions, BUT if their words and behavior are not in sync, they will join the thousands who have gone to their grave never knowing what they could have achieved with their life.

*Behavior Never Lies!* Beginning to understand the power in those three little words? Words are about establishing intentions. If those intentions are never implemented, they become a lie one keeps telling self. That lie will exhaust one; those contradictions will wear on their spirit. Over a period of time they will even become angry with self for talking about what they know they are not going to do.

*Behavior Never Lies!* Words that are spoken, but not acted on can cause others to lose faith and respect in a person. People who depend on a person listen to what they are saying. They hear and then watch to see what happens with the words.

If the words are not in sync with behavior, they soon don't believe what is being said.

Don't miss the power of those three little words – *Behavior Never Lies!*

Chapter 2

# The Circle Of Sameness

*People aren't because they are; they are because they are giving permission to be that way.*

Peggy looked at me with tears streaming down her face. "Richard, I am trapped, and I don't like it. I fight so hard to get out of this hole I have created for myself, but the harder I try the deeper I sink into this abyss. I want out!"

Steven sat in the seminar and I knew he was wrestling with what I was talking about. My message had been about taking control of one's environment and breaking free from the routines that trap us in sameness.

At the end of the program he was sitting there just staring at me. Finally, I looked at him and said, "Okay, it is apparent you are struggling with what I was talking about. Share with me what you are thinking."

My statement caught him off guard and for a moment he was just silent. Finally, he looked around and realized I was waiting for him to answer. "You're right. I am really struggling with what you were saying. I know what you are saying is correct, but I just can't see your teachings happening in any aspect of my life."

"Why?"

"I am not in control of the environment I am working in. Yes, I am the manager, but I have a manager above me who doesn't agree with the things we are being taught in these meetings. I come to these training classes and get excited because I see how this information can make us better. Then, I go back, share with the General Manager what I would like to do and hear him say, *This is just more corporate crap. We are not going to do it. What we are doing is okay.* I walk out of his presence feeling defeated. How do you take control of an environment when the people above you don't want the same thing? That is where I am challenged with what you are saying. I am trapped between what I know needs to be done and what

I am allowed to do. So, what do I do? I keep doing the things that are and have been frustrating me. I feel paralyzed. I don't like this feeling."

He was correct. He was trapped in an environment that was a contradiction. On one hand they talk about making improvements and that everything is on the table and open for discussion. Then, insights are shared and the people see how it can improve the environment, BUT are told by managers, who want to hold onto the status quo, "They can't use what they are being taught." The contradiction paralyzes the people and sends a negative message that negates the training.

Reeta and Charlie sat in front of me in silence. They would look at each other and then stare at me. Finally, I looked at them and said, "Okay, we have had a good look at each other. Now, what do we need to talk about? You called and asked if you could talk to me. So, we are all here; let's talk!"

They looked at each other and finally Charlie said, "Richard, we think our relationship is falling apart. We have been married for twelve years and lately we have really been at odds with each other. I don't think I know Reeta anymore."

At this point Reeta entered the conversation. "It is like we are strangers. We used to do so much together, and now we just sit home and stare at each other. We used to talk about everything, but now we seem to argue about every little thing. I don't like this feeling and I don't think I like what is happening to us."

They both looked at each other and Charlie continued. "We have become roommates, rather than husband and wife. We live in this draining routine that just seems to be sucking the life out of both of us. If we don't do something, it is going to destroy our marriage. Neither of us wants that. Can you help us get out of this sinkhole?"

Stories like these are not the exception; they are the rule. Over the years I have found that most people feel trapped in their life. Their life has become a routine that has stolen their inner spirit. As much as they want to break free, they are trapped in a repetitive circle that is daily stealing their life. They are trapped in the Circle of Sameness. What people fail to realize is they are not trapped by the situation; they are trapped by the behavior they have evolved to. They are trapped by the behavior they have made acceptable, even though they continually talk the desire to get out of it. Their words say one thing, but their behavior tells the real story.

---

The Circle of Sameness is not about what one's life is handed; it is about the behavior one brings to the events and situation their life is going through. The challenge is most don't interpret the situation of life with their mind; they view life's events through their emotions. That means rather than looking for a solution, they are looking for reasons and in many cases someone or something to blame. As long as one is looking for a reason or something or someone to blame, they are trapped.

---

Reacting to life is controlled by one's emotional interpretation. As long as life is being viewed from a picture of wrong, a person will only see what is wrong. The result is behaviors designed to trap them in a world of sameness. That sameness will constantly steal one's inner energy and leave them feeling there is no way out. When one feels there is no way out, they repeat the behaviors they know are wrong, but feel there is nothing they can do about it.

Tragic, but true – most people live their life going from

26

bad to worse. They expect things to go wrong and go about seeking the wrong in order to justify their behavior. Each time they find something that is going wrong it feeds their belief and feeling that this is the way their life is always going to be. Responding is also controlled by one's behavior. The difference between a life that is positive and growing and one that is negative and deteriorating is what they are looking for. Every choice they make is filled with emotions and thought. When the two come together they create one's feelings, which are implemented through behavior.

Responding occurs when positive emotions and positive thoughts come together to seek a solution that allows one to break free and move forward. When one is responding, their behavior assures them they will move through whatever part of life they are standing in.

Reacting occurs when negative emotions overpower a person's thoughts and seeks reasons, excuses or justification for what is happening in their life. When one reacts, they insure they will repeat the behaviors that are creating their repetitive draining lifestyle. The result is a life trapped in the Circle of Sameness.

This Circle of Sameness is such a draining place to live. It is about a repetitive lifestyle that continues the miss-beliefs one has been telling self. The Circle of Sameness is a routine set in place by blame, reasons and/or justification. It is a lifestyle controlled by behaviors designed to keep a person existing in a frustrating circle. This Circle of Sameness uses a family of negative emotions to keep one trapped in a routine existence where they can't see the exit. We've seen this behavior.

How many:

- wanna be's have we known?

- planners who never work their plan have we known?

- procrastinators have we known?

- conversations have we had with people where they talk about what they are going to do?

- conversations have we had with people who talk about the opportunities they have missed?

- times have we listened to people talk about how unfair their life has been?

- excuses, reasons and justifications have we listened to as the reason one's life is so messed up?

The Circle of Sameness is the biggest trap people get caught in. Yes, most would like to have more from their life, but they don't want to change anything to have it. It is easier to excuse, reason away or justify what they don't have. Very few will step forward and admit they are because of what they aren't willing to do. To face their Circle of Sameness they would have to be accountable for their behaviors and face the fact they choose each day to continue them.

Being trapped in the Circle of Sameness is not a happening; it is a choice. A person chooses the direction for their life. One acts out their life plan through behaviors each and every day. As much as one talks about wanting out, their behaviors insures they will remain trapped in the Circle. Don't forget – *behavior never lies.*

Breaking out of the Circle of Sameness is about ONE facing their life with honesty. What a challenge this is for most. Inwardly there is this desire to break out, but their behaviors are controlled by their negative fear that keeps raising its ugly head each time there is a possibility of breaking free. Because they have lived trapped for so long, it has become routine to give into the way things have always been.

Peter came to me seeking help. He was trapped in a life that was dragging him down. My question to him was, "Peter, can you handle honesty?"

The look on his face was a huge question mark. He just sat there and stared at me.

"This is the starting point. If you can't handle honesty, there is no way to move your life forward. Peter, most people create the lies that hold them hostage and then use excuses, reasons and justification as their validation point. Now, can you handle honesty?"

"Richard, I really don't know. I want to say yes, but I am not sure. I know I have lied to myself and used those lies as my reasons for not doing anything. I will tell you yes, I can handle honesty and if you see me wrestling with what you say or ask, you will know why."

Over the years I have learned that most remain trapped because they can't handle the honesty that is necessary to break free from their Circle of Sameness. I've found, most want honesty as long as it is not honest. Most are willing to face their life as long as their problem is someone else's fault. When it becomes "their" issue, they are not sure they want to deal with it. Over the years I have had so many come asking me to be their personal mental coach. The journey was fun until it came time to strip away the lies and face their life with honesty. Many have told me "Richard, this is too tough. I can't do this." With that their journey toward the freedom they said they wanted ends, and they retreat back into their Circle of Sameness.

Personal honesty is one of the toughest challenges a person can ask any person to go through. Why? It is about facing self. It is about removing the blame, the reasons and the excuses from one's life. It is about standing in front of one's personal viewing mirror and making self responsible for "what is." It is about fully understanding and accepting *Behavior Never Lies!*

Let me go back to a thought I introduced earlier – *a person is perfectly designed to achieve what they are achieving.* Life is the result of the choices one has made and implemented through their behavior. No one forces one to be the way they are; it is their choice. If one can't face and admit that, they will never break free from their Circle of Sameness.

Why is personal honesty such a challenge for people? It means once they have faced the issue, now they have to do something about it. It is about personal accountability. If one faces their life and don't do anything about it, they have not really faced their life. They have only stared at what they need to do. The result is the continuation of "what has been," not the "freedom to see" what their life can actually be.

The difference between facing an issue and staring at an issue is taking action. This is where many fall down. They know what they need to do; talk self into doing it and then, when it comes time to take action, they have a reason or an excuse for not doing it right now. They are going to do it, but just not right now. They will swear it will be done, but each time they are questioned, they have a reason why, "This is not a good time."

This becomes their pattern of living. Their life becomes a series of personal conversations about improving their life that never happens. They will share what they need to do, but create a time line that is somewhere in the future. Their statements of good intentions makes their behavior of not doing anything okay. They don't want to hear that good intentions are nothing more than a lie used to give them permission to postpone taking action.

Ralph is a perfect example. He is smart and very talented, but loaded with excuses. He will have conversation after conversation with people and share with them in detail what he needs to do to break free of his Circle of Sameness. The conversations are right on, but he never implements the needed action.

The last time we talked I told him, "Ralph, you are wasting my time."

The look on his face told me I had taken him by surprise. "What are you talking about?"

"I'm tired of these repetitive conversations. Each time we talk you share what you need to do to get your life out of the muck. We agree on a plan, and then, you walk out and never do one thing we have talked about. As far as I am concerned, you are lying to yourself and me. I don't want to have this conversation again."

"You mean you are giving up on me?" he said in a very angry tone.

"I'm not giving up on you. I am simply refusing to support your lies. If and when you are ready to do what you have said you are going to do, I am here for you. Until that point, I don't have the time or the energy to invest in your self destructive behavior."

Since that conversation, I have not heard from him. I have heard from others that he doesn't understand how I could treat him that way. He has told others, "I deserted him."

Ralph is not the only one like that. Many people talk a good story, but when it comes to taking action, they just don't do it. They know the right words; they understand what they need to do, but without implementing the right behavior it is all a lie. They need to understand *Behavior Never Lies.*

As long as one is repeating the behaviors of yesterday, they have to repeat yesterday. It makes no difference how much they talk about what they are going to do; until they take the correct action, they are trapped in their Circle of Sameness.

Emotionally wrestling with these people is a waste of energy. They know what they are doing, but have created their justifications. If one tries to talk to them about their inconsistency, they will play dumb or plead ignorance. They will accuse others of not supporting them. Until they are ready to face their behavior, their personal lie will keep them trapped in "what is."

The worse thing one can do for these people is support their personal lie. As long as a person gives them permission to continue their personal lie, they will. They must be held accountable; there must be consequences to their behavior; they must have to face their life with personal honesty. Supporting their personal lie makes one a participant in it. At some point they will turn on those who have been a part of their lie and blame them for what is wrong with their life. After all others didn't force them to confront their life. To them that meant they felt they were okay.

They must hold them accountable for what they are doing. Don't accept their excuses; question their behavior. Don't participate in their lie; call their attention to the contradiction. Keep the three little words, *Behavior Never Lies*, in front of them.

Mary was so red she looked like she was going to explode. She didn't have to tell me, but she did. "I am so angry at Mike. I have had it; I mean really had it. I know, I have told you that before, but Richard, this time I really mean it. I am so tired of listening to his lies. I have tried everything I know and nothing I say, do or threaten to do makes any difference."

Mike was such an interesting person. He had the personality that could charm a snake into being gentle. He had survived in life through his personality and his ability to make people believe he meant what he said. Reality was, he was the great pretender.

Mary had carried the financial load of the family for over three years. The company Mike had worked for went bankrupt, and Mike had been without work since then. Mary and Mike are not a one-income family. They had debt and Mary's salary wouldn't cover everything. They had talked and talked about the need for Mike to find a job. He kept telling her he was going to. He would look, but nothing was ever the "right job." All Mary saw was them slipping deeper and deeper into this pit. She had pushed, pulled, and threatened without any positive result from Mike.

Reality was, he enjoyed the life he had now. He could sleep in, get up when he wanted and have his coffee while reading the paper. Oh, he would get up with Mary, but the minute she left for work he was back in bed. He didn't help around the house, but complained to Mary about how messy the house was.

When she would get real angry, he would go on a job interview, but there was always some issue with that job. In the beginning Mary had told him, "Take your time. Don't just rush into any old job. Make sure it is the right one for you."

Little did she know he would take her words and use them against her. So many times he would remind her of her words. "Why are you so upset? You told me to take my time and find the right job. I am looking, but I just haven't found the right job yet."

She had had all of that she could handle. The night she was in my office I could tell she was at the end of her rope. "He has got to get off his lazy butt and help me. I can't, no I won't carry this load alone. Richard, I never thought I would say this, but I would be better off without him. I never thought I could imagine my life without him, but I don't like this person he has become. I look at him and find myself filled with rage. Some days I just want to hit him over and over. That is not me. I don't like this person I am turning into. I just look at him and get angry. Help me!"

I scheduled a meeting with Mike, and when he showed up, he looked at me and said, "I guess Mary has been talking to you."

"Yes, we have talked. Mike, you know she is totally frustrated with you."

"Yea! She tells me that. I understand part of why she is frustrated, but on the other hand I am confused by her behavior."

"Why are you confused?"

"Well, when I lost my job, she told me she didn't want me to hurry and just get something I wasn't going to be happy doing. I thought she meant that, but I guess those were just words."

"No, I think she was serious. I just don't think she thought you would go this long without finding a job."

" I know it has been a long time, but I just can't seem to find something I enjoy. I have been looking, but nothing has hit my fancy."

"Do you understand the financial pressure Mary feels?"

"Yes, I hear about that all the time. I know it is stressing her out, but what am I suppose to do?"

"Mike, I have a serious question for you. Are you really looking for a job or have you become comfortable not working?"

There was this long pause and a look that said I didn't have the right to ask that question. The tone changed as he replied, "Yes, I am looking for a job, but I am not going to just take anything."

"Then, explain to me what you are looking for."

"You know!"

"No, I don't know. Tell me what you are looking for."

"I want a job where I can be happy."

"What does that mean?"

"You know; something that makes me want to go to work."

"What kind of a job would that be."

"I'm not sure. I just know I haven't found it yet."

"Mike, I don't think you are being honest with yourself. You like the way your life is right now. You have it made. You get up, watch Mary go to work and then you just do your thing. That is a great life. From what I hear you don't help with things around the house. You are there all day, but the house is Mary's job. Is that correct?"

"Why should I do anything around the house? Nothing

35

I do is good enough. When I do try to help, she comes in, complains about it not being done correct and re-does it. So, I just decided I wouldn't do anything."

"Do you think it is possible she complains because she is frustrated with you? Could it be she is tired of going to work and knowing that you are at home being lazy and not working to help her by getting a job?"

There was nothing but silence from him. I could tell he didn't like this conversation and didn't want it to go any further.

"Mike, you are trapped in this routine you have created for yourself. You tell yourself you want a job, but you don't. You tell yourself you know you need to go back to work, but you are using the lack of being able to find the perfect job as your excuse. You are not seeing what this is doing to your relationship. Mary has been very patient, but she is reaching the end of her rope. She is almost at the point where she has had enough. If you let her get to that point, you won't have to worry about your marriage. It will be over."

He leaned back, looked at me and laughed. "She wouldn't do that. She loves me and wouldn't know what to do without me. I am her anchor."

"Yes! You have become the anchor around her neck. Listen to me and hear what I am saying. She is close to cutting the rope. She has sharpened the knife and is sitting trying to finalize her decision. You can stop all this by changing your behavior. You can stop this madness by proving to her you care. All you have to do is get a job. That will prove to her you are serious about helping her and the relationship."

I paused, leaned in and looked him squarely in the eyes. "Mike, do you hear what I am saying? This is not a game.

This is a very serious time in your relationship. You have to break out of this dangerous circle you have not only created for yourself, but spend each day justifying. Mary is no longer going to listen to what you say. You have got to step up to the plate with a new behavior. You have to stop talking about what you are going to do, stop using her words against her and do what you know you need to do. You know my three words of life, don't you?"

The look on his face said he was getting it. "Yes, I know your three words – *Behavior Never Lies*."

"Then, answer this question for yourself, not me – have you been lying to yourself and Mary about looking for a job?"

The Circle of Sameness goes against a person's inner spirit. The inner spirit doesn't want to be trapped. One's inner spirit doesn't want to live trapped in sameness. It wants to be free to explore. It wants to seek out possibilities and explore them. When one agrees to and lives in their Circle of Sameness, they take away the meaning of life.

It is so easy to get trapped in this Circle. It is so easy to bring it to one's life and then justify living trapped in repetitive behavior. How many times does a person justify it through good intentions? They talk about what they are going to do, or about what they should do, or what they will do when, or about what they will do if, BUT all the words are just a lie. They make those statements hoping others will think they are really going to do something. In the beginning they may believe what the person is saying, but over a period of time when they don't see any positive action, they stop believing what the person is saying or has said.

The Circle of Sameness shuts down one's imagination. One's life is about creating; it is about seeing the opportunities in today; it is about having a dream that fills a person's life with energy. All of this happens in one's imagination. When they make the Circle of Sameness a lifestyle, their imagination shuts down. Without their imagination their dream stops sketching the world of opportunity; without their dream they have no direction; without direction life's events don't have a positive connection point; without these connection points a person is trapped in repeating a yesterday that exhausts and frustrates them. Is that really living? Is this really something one would choose for their life?

Don't forget, *Behavior Never Lies*.

Chapter 3

# Accountability

*Repeating behaviors that hold you hostage will insure you can't move beyond your yesterday.*

Behavior Never Lies!  BUT if behavior is never challenged, it is validated. I have found it interesting how much easier it is to criticize a person than it is to talk to them about their behavior. When one's behavior isn't challenged, the silence validates the behavior. The lack of confrontation sends a message of acceptance. When they feel their behavior is validated, there is no reason to do anything about it and no understanding when one finally gets fed up and attacks them with what they have done and/or are not doing.

What ever happened to holding people accountable for their behavior? Why has blame become an acceptable defense for wrong behavior? Why will a person sit and not express their feelings when they know those feelings are going to cause internal anguish?

We seem to be a society that has cracked at its very fiber. So much of what our nation was built on has been thrown out. We have become a society that justifies wrongs, refuses to stand up for beliefs and is guided by a misconception that good will win in the end.

Reality is *if there is not a foundation to hold us together, we will fall apart while we are blaming everything for it.*

All Janice ever wanted was to be a teacher. From her early years in school all she talked about was being a teacher. All the time she was in high school and college, she couldn't wait to get out and get into the classroom.

She came to me after her third year of teaching frustrated, stressed and angry. She started talking before she got into my office. "If I cry, don't pay any attention. I am just so angry and disappointed I don't know what to do."

She paused, as I pointed her to a chair that she clasped

into. I looked at her and in her eyes was this look of sadness. "Janice, tell me what's going on?"

"All I've ever wanted to do is teach. It is what I have been living for, but I've got to tell you what I am doing is not teaching. I have been trained to challenge children's minds and help prepare them for life, BUT I am nothing more than a glorified babysitter. Richard, I am so frustrated."

"Okay, slow down. Let's walk through this together. I've known you since high school, and all I've heard you talk about is your desire to be a teacher. I have been so amazed at how focused you have been. Walk me through what is creating all this frustration in you."

"First, is the school system. It really isn't designed to let you teach. You really don't have control of your classroom. You can't discipline a child without paying a severe consequence. I don't feel I have the support of the administration. Let me give you an example. I have four students in my class that can't read and can't spell. I think they need to be held back for one year. When I talked to the administration, I was told we don't do that. They said there were too many social ramifications that go with holding them back. I wanted to know if passing the children to the next grade wasn't a lie. They are not ready and passing them on is not helping them; it is hurting them. We need to hold them accountable for their learning, but we choose to just pass them on and lie to them. That is not right."

"Janice, you are not going to get an argument from me. I have preached for years that we are giving kids a piece of paper, telling them they are educated when they are not. I agree with you here. What else is frustrating you?"

"Parents! I don't think many of them really care about

what or how their child is doing in school. Recently, I had a parent-child conference. I have thirty-five children in my room. How many parents do you think showed up to talk with me about their child?"

"Well, let me see. I would say about half."

"I would have been happy with half. Out of thirty-seven children, only five parents showed up. FIVE! It has been that way for three years now. Don't they care about how their children are doing in school? Oh, if there is a problem where their kid gets called on the carpet, they will be there. Not to find out what happened, but to blame the system for the issue their child had."

She shook her head, looked at me with fire in her eyes and continued. "I'll give you a good example. Not long ago I had a child in my class walk up to another child and hit him with a book. I mean rare back and hit him in the face with a book. When I questioned him as to why he did it, he told me he didn't like the way the other student had looked at him in the hall. Well, fighting is an automatic three-day suspension. The next day I had a visit from the parents who wanted to know why their child had been suspended for three days. As I was trying to explain what had happened, the mother stood up, walked over, put her finger in my face and in a screaming voice wanted to know why I was out to get her child. I tried to explain to her that I wasn't, but she didn't want to hear that. She was going to the principal and have me fired. I just looked at her and realized why her son was the way he was. Why couldn't she just work with me and together use this as a lesson for her son? No, she didn't want to hear what her son had done; she didn't want to make him responsible or hold him accountable for his action. How is this child ever going to learn with parents like this? When they left, I was so angry. It was all I could do to hold my temper."

She paused, looked me squarely in the eyes and said, "This is not teaching. This is babysitting. I didn't spend all those years in school to stand in a classroom and not be able to teach. I am not sure this is what I want to do anymore. Without accountability in the school system there isn't any education."

What happens if a child grows up not having to be accountable for their behavior? What happens when they can do what they want and have their parents protect them, even when they are wrong? What kind of a message does that send?

Studying the behavior of a child, gives a picture of their parents. Put a child in an accountability driven environment that has never been taught accountability, what's going to happen? They are going to resist the authority and refuse to follow the rules they are given. Children need parents, not playmates. Homes need to teach accountability, rather than send a message that tells the child to resist authority.

Marion came to me in a state of depression and despair. She was the membership director for a country club and really enjoyed her job. I could see why. She was a people person. I am not sure she ever met a stranger. Her personality and her belief in the club made her a great ambassador. She had called me while I was on the road and asked if we could talk as soon as I got back in town. I could tell by her voice something major was wrong, so we arranged to meet for dinner.

I arrived early and she was already there. "I'm not use to people beating me to a meeting," I said with a big grin on my face.

She forced a smile and said, "I needed to get away from the club, so I thought I would just come and sit until you got here. I really appreciate you taking your time to meet with me."

"Hey, you said you needed to talk and your tone told me this was not going to be a casual conversation."

"They fired me!"

"They what?"

"Richard, my regional manager fired me."

"What happened?"

"In October the head golf pro came to me and asked if I wanted in on a thing they were doing. You know that for holiday gifts some members buy gift certificates. The reality is not many of the gift certificates are ever used. What the golf pro and the assistant shop manager were doing was keeping a list of all the gift certificates that were sold and then, when they weren't used, they were cashing them in and taking the money in the form of merchandise and selling it to other people. They wanted to cut me in. I told them no. I didn't know what to do, so I called the Regional Manager and shared with him what they were doing. He told me not to tell anyone and he would see me the following week. He called the following Wednesday and asked if we could meet that afternoon."

The look on her face was one of disbelief. "When we sat down to talk this is what he said to me, *Marion, you have put me in a tough situation. I agree what these guys are doing is not correct. My dilemma is I either have to fire my golf pro and assistant shop manager or fire you.* I couldn't believe what I was hearing. I asked him why he would have to fire me. I hadn't done anything wrong. All I was doing was telling him what they were doing. It wasn't right. They were stealing. He told me, *if I fire them, I would have to replace a damn good golf pro and a very good shop manager. They would be real difficult to replace. When I look at the situation, you would be the easiest to replace.*

There was a long moment of silence. She turned away to wipe her eyes, looked at me and continued. "So, he fired me. The reason he gave was the lack of membership growth. He said I wasn't doing the job of selling memberships that I needed to be doing. He then talked to the two guys and told them they had to stop their gift certificate scam. I can't believe he would allow them to stay when there were stealing from the company and fire me for trying to do the right thing. Where's the right in this? Why did I get punished and them get rewarded? Isn't there any accountability left in the business world?"

> Behavior is a fact; accountability is a choice. Without accountability there are no rules and anything goes. Without accountability there is no consequence to what one does. When that is true, people are free to do what they want without any punishment for their wrong behavior.

What has happened to us? What has happened to our moral fiber? Where have our ethics gone?

When we look at situations like Enron, World Com and the others who have stolen from people who trusted them, taken from people who had invested their life savings in these companies and watched as the thieves keep their fortunes and those who had trusted them lost everything. Where is the accountability? Where is the right in this? How can a legal system make this okay?

What has happened to a society that makes wrong right and right something a person gets punished for. What has happened to the Golden Rule? How can stealing and lying be justified? When wrong is made right and there is no consequence for behavior, then anything goes.

I was working with an organization that had made accountability their major theme for their new mission. The new Executive Director followed a gentleman who had been in place for over thirty years and he didn't allow anyone to make a decision. He controlled everything. If someone didn't like it, they didn't have to work there. What did this do to the people in the environment? There were people with a "management" title, but did no real managing. They were simply task directors.

When he retired and Allan was hired as the new Executive Director, he inherited a very dysfunctional environment where people showed up, went through their routine, didn't care how they did what they did and everyone had and did their own agenda.

When Allan called me and asked if I would help him turn this place around, my question to him was simple, "Are you up to this challenge?"

There was silence followed by a chuckle. "I hope so. I know this is not going to be easy. I spent a month with him studying what he did. It was so frightening. The people feared him; his directors had no voice and management was non-existent. He was everything I don't want to be and pray I never become."

One can just imagine what the environment was like. There was no "togetherness;" there were lots of mistakes that punished their customers and no one seemed to care if a mistake was made. Most people showed up and just did what they defined their job to be.

Allan is a person who believes in allowing people to do their job. He also believes that the crusade of an organization is to take care of their customers. Anytime the customer is confused or disappointed with their experience, it is a statement about the lack of internal concern, which is demonstrated through a behavior that says "we don't care." That was something Allan had never tolerated anywhere he had been. In reality he was hired because of his intense commitment to taking care of the customer.

His first challenge was Arthur. Arthur was second in command and had been there almost as long as the gentleman Allan replaced. Arthur just knew he would be given the Executive Director's job. The Board had decided they needed someone completely different, so that eliminated Arthur from consideration.

Put yourself in Arthur's situation. He had waited for most of his adult working years for the position of Executive Director. Then, when the time arrived, they didn't even consider him. What should Arthur do? He could leave, but where could he go at his age that would pay him what he was making? He could retire, but he was too young and needed to work a few more years. So, the only real option he had was to stay. That was a huge emotional issue. Arthur knew he should have had the job; he knew Allan had come in and taken what should have been his. How could he give Allan his full support, when he had his job!

What an emotional mess for Allan. He inherited a second in command who was filled with jealousy and anger. Here is Allan, the "new" guy, having to depend on a person who didn't like him without even knowing him. Yes, Allan could fire him, but what kind of message would that send to the rest of the troops.

Then, there were Allan's Direct Reports. Here was a tremendous talent pool that had been put on the shelf. They were bright, but their light had been dimmed by a person who was a dictator, not a leader. Their only value was fighting fires, not providing leadership. They really were caring people, but anytime they had expressed a caring spirit, they had been punished. The result was a diminishing of their caring; they saw what needed to be done, but knew if they approached the Executive Director, they would be punished for wanting to step on his kingdom.

Enter Allan, who was not a dictator. Allan was a person who felt that with the leadership position came the responsibility to make decisions. He was also a person who didn't step over or around his leadership partners. He expected them to do what needed to be done; yes, he wanted to know what was going on, but he didn't want to have to do it for them.

How uncomfortable did that make his Direct Reports? Should they believe him? Should they trust that he wasn't setting them up to pull the rug out from under them? They decided to take a wait and see attitude. They would listen to what he said, BUT they would continue to do what they had always done and see what happened.

Now, add to this Allan's department managers. Here was a group that had had a position, but no direction. Here was a group that had a title, but no authority. They had grown accustomed to just coming to work, going through the task of shuffling paper and not being held accountable for anything that created confusion in their department. The agenda was whatever they decided it would be. Now, this new Executive Director walks in and starts talking about accountability. He talked about them being responsible for the behavior of the people in their department. Think these people weren't fearful? They were being asked to do things they had never done before. They were asked to step up and stop managing tasks and start leading people. Most of them had no people training and didn't have the confidence needed to face the issues that had become a common negative part of their department.

So when Allan called me and asked if I would help him redesign this environment, my first question was, "Do you know what you have gotten yourself into?" I asked him. "I have to be sure you are committed to being there. Nothing would be worse than starting these people on a journey and then leaving them hanging out there. Allan, do you feel this is where you are meant to be?"

He assured me it was and that he was there for the long haul. That started a journey with Allan and I committed to building the people through a program of personal development. The journey started with his second in command. We needed to see where his loyalty was. Was he committed to working with Allan or working his own agenda behind the scenes? Allan and I talked about raising the stakes and making sure where his second was in his commitment. Slowly, but surely Arthur's presence started showing that he was on board with Allan and wanted to be a strength in the journey. His behavior said, "I have my own agenda, but I am willing to give this a try." His behavior created a concern we knew we would have to revisit.

The next step was his Direct Reports. This group was as important, if not more important, than the second in command. These were actually the people Allan had to work through. These were his lifelines to his managers who were the lifeline to the people. These Directs had to be onboard if things were going to improve.

With the help of Susie, the Training Director, a

retreat was designed where the agenda was to challenge the commitment of the people. It was apparent there was confusion, skepticism and even conflict between those who made up this group. The retreat was a success and this group of talented people came back united in their commitment to the organization. Reality was, they still weren't 100% sure of Allan. Allan and I talked about this being a time of patience and consistency. He had to patiently show them through his consistent behavior that he was real and didn't have any hidden agendas. Through his patient consistent persistency he won them over. Now, with them and Arthur behind him, the journey could reach down into his department managers.

This was a tougher sell. These people were knowledgeable in their areas, but not trained in the leadership skills they needed to work with people. My mission was to challenge their comfortable routines, expose their fears and provide them with the people skills to move from a task manager to the leader of their people. Within three months Allan and I began to see the emotional walls come down. Yes, they were still fearful, but they were at least willing to face their fears. Yes, they were uncertain about what was going on, but they were willing to listen. No, they didn't understand all they were being taught, but most of them were willing to admit what they didn't know and continue to challenge themselves.

On several occasions I talked about the fact *you are not tested while you are learning; the test comes when you know what to do and come face to face with a situation that demands you use it.* I talked to them about the fear that goes with implementing something that causes a leader to have to confront people they have been passive with. We talked about that in that moment the person would know whether they were a leader or not.

It didn't take long for two major tests to surface. I found out a long time ago when a negative person's comfortable routine is challenged, they will push to see if the leader is real or just blowing hot air.

The first challenge came with a lady who came back from lunch with the smell of alcohol on her breath. This was not the first time it had happened, and she would brag about her drinking at lunch. There was a policy in place that stated, "drinking, while on the job, was grounds for disciplinary action, and if the situation continued, it was grounds for dismissal."

Since the environment had been task driven and not people oriented, nothing had ever been done. In the new design the behavior was not acceptable. When she was confronted, she immediately screamed she was being unjustly singled out and ran to her union steward. Now, the test was in place. Would the leadership cave into the pressure of the union or stand its ground with the new design? Allan and his Directors saw the challenge and stood united in their commitment to enforce the rules that all the people had agreed to. They took the union on and won! What a powerful message that sent throughout the organizational environment. It sent a very loud message that we are moving into a new time and accountability will be a big part of what we do.

Shortly after this incident, a second situation surfaced that provided even a bigger test for the commitment of the leadership partners to the crusade of redesign and accountability. In one department there was a lady who had severe allergies. She was especially sensitive to certain perfume scents. Another lady in the department wore a perfume that contained the scent the lady was allergic to. The manager approached her, explained the situation to her and asked if she would mind not wearing that particular perfume. Rather than responding with a positive, she reacted to the request and wore even more of the perfume.

A solution had to be reached. When it was apparent the lady was not going to honor the request, the decision was made to move the department. This was not a reaction; the department had been planned to move. The timetable was just adjusted.

So, the twenty people were moved to another area. Well, the lady who refused to not wear the perfume and another of her friends decided to get back at the lady with the allergies. They took their perfume, sprayed it on real strong and went to the area where the other lady sat.

It happened that Arthur was walking down the hallway and saw the lady with the allergies gasping for breath. When she didn't seem to be getting any better, Arthur decided he had better take her to the hospital. Once outside in the fresh air, she was able to get her breath. When she explained to Arthur what had happened, he immediately decided the situation had to be confronted. His first stop was with the Union Steward. When it was explained to the Steward what had happened, the Steward agreed the behavior of the two ladies needed to be confronted.

In our manager's meeting the question was posed to me, "How should we handle this?"

My response was, "This was an ugly behavior that was planned and carried out without any regard for the lady with allergies. The consequences here must send a message that states in no uncertain terms this behavior will not be tolerated here. The two should be confronted in a meeting with the entire department. The question to them is very simple. Why did you spray the perfume and go to her work area?"

The look on several of the manager's faces was one of disbelief. One manager blurted out, "You can't do that. That will embarrass these two ladies."

I paused, looked at both of them and responded. "Different types of behaviors demand different levels of responses. If their behavior had been an accident, I would take them aside and confront them in private, BUT this was no accident. This was premeditated and done with malicious intent. This was an ugly action done by two people demonstrating an ugly behavior. Their behavior demands a stronger confrontation. With the way it happened, they couldn't say it was an accident. They knew what they were doing and chose to do it. This was simply mean and very dangerous."

I was amazed how several of the managers thought it would be wrong to address them in public. Yes, they felt they should be talked to, but not in front of the entire group. Yes, they agreed the action was deliberate, but just because they chose to do it, didn't mean they should be embarrassed in front of the entire group.

When I asked them, "How would you handle it so the message was sent that all people will be accountable for their behavior?" They didn't have a plan.

If a person chooses to act in a way they know is wrong and could be dangerous to another person, they must be held accountable. Here these people were striving to redesign an environment where the message had been "anything goes" and now the new message is "people will be held accountable for their behavior." Here are two women who knowingly decided to disregard the safety of another person and act out an ugly behavior. The incident was not a secret; it was known all over the building. All eyes were on the Leadership group. If they did nothing, all they were striving to do would be viewed as a lie. If they did very little, it would send a message they weren't serious about the accountability statement they had made. This was a test that couldn't be taken for granted.

My next question to the managers was, "What message do you want sent to the entire group? When management is tested, they must respond, not react. Their behavior must not be seen as out of control."

When Arthur was talking about the situation, he said, "My first reaction was to go in and rip their heads off. I just couldn't believe they could be that insensitive to another person's situation. I thought about what we have been discussing in these meetings and decided it was not the right action. So, I slowed down, thought and decided the first step was to go to the Union Steward and get his support. I couldn't believe it when he agreed with my thinking that this was a major wrong."

Arthur showed a lot of maturity. He, first of all, held himself accountable for his behavior. Too many times people hold others accountable, but not self. That contradiction destroys the message they are trying to convey.

Still, there was resistance to taking a public action. Many still thought it would be wrong to confront them in front of the group. I thought it was time to raise the intent of the lesson that had to be understood. This was too important to soften the message.

"If you don't make a powerful statement, you validate their behavior. You must understand it is not the people we are going after; we are challenging their behavior. You must learn how to confront behavior and still love people. You must learn how to hold people accountable for their behavior without destroying the person. Your challenge with this is your fear of people not liking you for what you are doing. Leadership is not about people liking you; it is about creating an environment that confronts behavior and holds people accountable for their actions. It is about creating presence through respect. For years you have been taught your job is dealing with tasks. That is no longer your major responsibility. You have been promoted from Task Master to Environmental Leader. If you can't handle the promotion, you need to rethink your position."

I think increasing the stakes shocked several of them. They were not ready for that level of accountability.

One of the managers finally said what I knew was going through so many of their heads. "This is not what we are use to. We have been taught to leave the people alone and just deal with the problems that arise. Now, you are telling us to deal with the people. I think managing tasks is a lot easier than leading people."

How true her words were. Managing tasks are always easier than leading people. A person can shuffle paper and feel like they have accomplished something.

Leading people is another issue. To lead people the leader has to confront behavior. This is why so many leaders spend their time fighting fires. They concentrate on task and avoid people. In that scenario the issues never go away. Until the leader confronts the behavior of people, they give them permission to continue. Reality is the leader either confronts or validates! There is no middle ground. If the leader validates, they become a participant in the situation. If they confront, the leader establishes a presence as the leader.

Get the message? Improvement, behavior and

accountability are part of the same program of growth. Nothing can improve if behavior is not challenged and people held accountable for their behavior. Without accountability behavior has no boundaries. Without accountability those whose game playing is the strongest will control the environment. Without accountability there is no leadership; there are only participants who find themselves in constant battles over control of the environment.

This idea of improvement, behavior and accountability being tied together in the growth journey is not a new thought, BUT it is one that is constantly resisted. Why?

From the management ranks it is about the lack of experience and the lack of training, which creates the fears of rejection and failure. Both of these fears are hostage takers. They fill the person with doubt, worry and make them feel uncertain about almost everything they decide to do.

Too many of those who are given a management position are not really trained to deal with the people they are responsible for managing. Many are chosen because of their task skills with little consideration given to their people skills. That is okay until they come face to face with the behavior of people who make doing the task challenging. Then, the manager is stifled. Now a choice has to be made. They either face the person and challenge their behavior or they add their load to theirs and avoid the confrontation. What would most who lack experience and skills do? They avoid the person and try to work around their behavior. In doing so they strengthen the person they are working around and weaken their presence with their people. Once it is felt the manager is weak, they will be tested time and time again. Over a period of time this will wear them down and finally out.

This could be avoided if companies would understand the need to train their people to understand human behavior. Several years ago I had a CEO tell me, "All I want my management people to know is how to do the job. All this people stuff is over-rated. As long as they have the technical skills, they can handle the job."

Interesting, because my research revealed this company's greatest challenge was keeping managers and developing a strong leadership. The average manager lasted thirteen months. The result was a lack of consistency with their people and products. There was also inner turmoil that kept the plant in constant confusion. As I thought about all this, I couldn't help but chuckle. He had come to me because of the turnover issue, but refused to face what was creating the situation.

Show me any company that understands the power of behavior, and that's a company that prepares their managers with people skills, controls turnover and strengthens its profitability. Business is about producing a product, BUT the people produce that product. If there are people issues, there will be product issues. If there are people issues, there are management issues.

Yes, management has to be able to address and direct tasks, but more importantly they must be able to lead people. Without the leadership of people the environment will internally crumble.

This idea of improvement, behavior and accountability being tied together in the growth journey is not a new thought, BUT it is one that is constantly resisted. Why?

From the personal view it has become far too easy to blame others for what one doesn't want to face. When blame becomes an acceptable pattern of behavior, accountability goes out the window. When the logic of "it's not my fault" is not challenged, there is no control over behavior.

Eileen is a seventh grader who is in constant conflict at school. Her parents asked if I would visit with her and see if I could discover where the conflict was coming from. Our first visit was very interesting. Every time I asked Eileen a question her mother would answer.

I asked about homework and immediately the mother reacted with, "They just give them too much. We spend at least three hours a night doing homework. By the time we finish it is bed time."

When I asked Eileen about friends at school, the mother jumped in with, "She doesn't really have any close friends. The one's she does have live across town and there is no time to see them. I don't like her playing with the children in our neighborhood. They aren't a good influence for her."

This pattern continued through the entire hour. Even though I asked the mother to let Eileen talk, she couldn't stop her butting in. I decided the next visit would be just Eileen and I.

At our second meeting Eileen wanted to know why her mother wasn't in the room. I told her I needed to talk to her for a few minutes.

"Eileen, do you enjoy school?"

"I guess. I have subjects I like and subjects I don't like."

"What subjects do you like? What is your favorite subject?"

She thought for a moment and then replied, "I like art. I like to draw pictures. Some days we get to paint and I like that."

"Do you like your teachers?"

"I like all of them, but Mrs. Oliver."

"Why don't you like Mrs. Oliver?"

"She is mean to me. She doesn't like me."

"Why do you think Mrs. Oliver doesn't like you?"

"She picks on me."

"Mrs. Oliver picks on you? How does she do that?"

"She shouts at me in front of the other students. I was talking to Mary and she walked over and told me to be quiet. I wasn't talking loud."

"Should you have been talking in class?"

"I wasn't being bad. I just needed to tell Mary something. It was important."

"Do you talk a lot in class?"

"I don't know. Some times I guess I do."

"Has Mrs. Oliver ever sent a note home to your mother about you talking in class?"

"Yes. She sent one home the other day and my mom got mad."

"What did your mom say?"

"She said she was going to go talk to Mrs. Oliver. I told her I really didn't talk that much. I told her Mrs. Oliver was always screaming at me. I don't like it when she picks on me."

"Eileen, think with me. Does Mrs. Oliver really scream at you? Does your mom ever scream at you?"

"Yes! Mom screams a lot. She is always upset at someone or something. When she is upset, she screams and that is almost all the time."

"Now, think about how your mom screams. Is that what Mrs. Oliver does to you?"

Eileen dropped her head and with her eyes focused on

the floor said, "No! She doesn't scream like mom screams."

"Eileen, could it be you are just upset with Mrs. Oliver because she doesn't want you to talk in class."

"I guess so. I know I'm not suppose to talk in class, but sometimes I just have to tell people something. It can't wait so I tell them."

I left Eileen in my office and walked out to her mother who was sitting in the foyer. I sat down beside her and calmly said, "Eileen is a sharp young lady. She is very intelligent and a master at telling stories the way she wants you to hear them."

Her mother looked at me with a smile on her face and said, "She really is a bright child. She walked early, started talking early and always seemed to be ahead of the others around her."

"Tell me about her teacher Mrs. Oliver."

"Oh, you mean the crabby one. She is not a good teacher. She is always sending notes home telling me something Eileen has done wrong. I don't think she likes Eileen. I have spoken to the principle about her, but it hasn't helped. I wanted to get Eileen in another classroom, but they said they were all full. Mrs. Oliver is not a good teacher."

"Does Eileen know how you feel about Mrs. Oliver?"

"Yes she does. I told her that Mrs. Oliver wasn't a good teacher and don't be worried about the notes she sends home. Eileen told me that Mrs. Oliver didn't like her and I agreed."

"Do you see anything wrong in telling Eileen that?"

"No, because it is the truth. That teacher doesn't like my daughter. She picks on her for things that any child does. Eileen loves to talk and I know she talks a lot in class, but what child doesn't. Eileen is not good with getting her homework done, but that is not as big an issue as Mrs. Oliver makes it to be. I work with her, and I know she knows the material. All kids struggle with homework. Eileen just doesn't have a long attention span. The teacher should understand that."

Unbelievable! Here is a seventh grader telling her out of control mother about her teacher and convincing her that the teacher doesn't like her. Here is a mother listening to her seventh grader and without talking to the teacher making the teacher the enemy. What message was that sending to Eileen? Does Eileen accept accountability as a fact of life?

What kind of respect will Eileen have for people who don't allow her to have her way? What kind of stories will Eileen tell her mother? Will Eileen always have someone or something to blame for the issues in her life?

How many Eileen's are coming from out of control homes today? What happens when a child doesn't have to be accountable for their behavior? Does that send a dangerous message about accountability to the child?

I am not sure where our society got off track with discipline, but without discipline there is no accountability. I'm sorry, but I don't think there is anything wrong with a smack on the butt of a child who is misbehaving. I am not talking about beating a child, but I am talking about a spanking that sends a message about acceptable and unacceptable behavior.

I am not talking about cruel punishment; I am talking about consequences for behavior. Look at our Juvenile Justice system today. A teenager can commit a crime and not have to suffer the consequences because of their age. They do wrong, know they have done wrong, but know they can get away with it. What reason is there not to do wrong when the child knows they are not going to be held accountable? What message does that send about behavioral consequences? Without accountability there are no rules! Without accountability anything goes.

Look at the parents who will deny the behavior of their child. They blame all aspects of society for the behavior of their child. When are we going to have an awakening? When are we going to look at the parents and hold them accountable for their lack of parental behavior?

We have become a society where no one is at fault. We have become a society that is unwilling to face the issues that are destroying our ethical and moral fiber; it is so much easier to blame and excuse. We excuse and say we are working on fixing the problem, rather than stepping up and facing the person's behavior. All situations are about people. All people are about behavior. Until there is accountability, anything goes. Until one is accountable for their behavior, there will always be reasons, excuses, blame and justification that make someone or something else responsible and the person not accountable. Reality is, *Behavior Never Lies*, but that seems to be a fact we don't want to accept.

Chapter 4

# Trust, Behavior & Contradictions

*When you trust you, your behaviors will
define that trust.*

I had finished my presentation with a network-marketing meeting in St. Louis and was in my booth outside the meeting room. There were several people lined up to talk to me, but one gentleman caught my eye. The expression on his face said he had something he needed to say. Finally, everyone was gone and he made his way toward me.

For a moment he just stood there looking at me. I knew he wasn't sure how to say what he wanted to say. "Looks like something is really playing in your head, but you are not sure how to say it," I said with a smile on my face. "I've been there and the best thing to do is just say it. I'll bet it will come out okay."

He smiled back and finally spoke up. "I bet you are right. I really enjoyed what you had to say, but there is one thing you said that I didn't agree with."

"Hey, I like it when people don't agree with me. It means they are listening and mentally working through my content. Tell me what you didn't agree with."

"Once I wouldn't have agreed with your statement *Behavior Never Lies*. Today I understand exactly what you are saying. Not long ago I trusted this man with some of my money and he lied to me. I feel I am a good judge of character and his behavior said I could trust him, but boy did I get taken. The opportunity I was offered sounded good, and I thought I did a great job of checking everything out, but once again I sat myself up. Right now I just want to give up on believing anyone means what they say."

"Listen to what you are saying. No doubt you are a good judge of character, but there are people who can fool all of us. I make my living being able to recognize behavior, but even I have been fooled. What you thought you saw through his behavior was a contradiction; it was a lie."

"I guess you are right. I have been beating myself over being so dumb."

"You weren't dumb; you were duped. You met a con artist. For many of us our basic instinct is to trust. When we do and get burned, we really feel dumb. The reality is you just didn't know the other person's full agenda. You didn't understand the real intent. What you have to learn is the fact that all behavior has an agenda. If you don't know the agenda, you are limited in your understanding. Confusion sets in when you are told one agenda and then find out it was a lie. The real intent was not the stated intent."

"I guess I need to become better at reading people."

"That would help, but the real message in this is to not forget the concept of agenda. I mean it when I say *all behavior has an agenda*. The agenda is the real intent. Dishonest people say one thing, but mean another. You have to slow down and see the real intent. That is what allows you to mentally see the total picture, rather than emotionally racing in and just accepting what you are seeing."

All behavior does have an agenda! There is really nothing that is spontaneous. Why, because all behavior takes thought. For action to take place it has to be emotionally pieced together and mentally given permission. This means all behavior has intent attached to it. It is the intent that creates the mission. Too many times the stated intent is not the real intent. We are fooled because we trust the person and then get disappointed when we find out we have been tricked.

How many times has a person bought into someone's pity story, helped and found out they had been used? How many times has a person had someone use their kindness and then get stabbed in the back?

Behavior has two sides. There is the side that is based in behavior one can believe, and then there is the side that is about the real intent. This is where the confusion comes in. These two can look the same, but have different agendas. How many times has one wanted to believe, but their gut was telling them to walk carefully? How many times has one raced in only to find their self caught in an agenda they weren't aware of?

Behavior that is based in love and caring doesn't play games. It is about one person reaching out through their hurt to help another.

Behavior that is deceptive creates the illusion of caring, but if one really studies what they are hearing with their ears and compare it to what they are seeing with their eyes, they will see the difference. The contradictions will be apparent and one can see through to the real agenda.

Many get caught in a game they are not even aware is being played. Anytime one is relying strictly on their emotions, they are setting self up to be used. Their emotions cannot give them the whole picture. Emotions can only build the picture on what one is feeling. Depending on a person's need level, those feelings can be misleading. They can want something so much, they create an unreal illusion they use to define what they feel is happening in their life. To base any decision strictly on emotions is not seeing the total picture.

Yet, at the same time one can't rely strictly on their mind. It is also limited when it comes to the total picture. One's mind can only deal with what they are thinking.

Thinking, too many times, is based on where one has been and what they have been through. One's mind is a reference library and each event they have been through creates a point of understanding for them. If their definition of "what was" is strictly understood by what they think they have learned, they can miss the total meaning of the event.

A person has to balance what they are feeling with what they are thinking. In doing so, they will slow down and listen with their eyes and ears. That is where they will see the total picture. They have to trust both their eyes and their ears. When they are working together, a person is on top of their game. They will see the total picture and aren't vulnerable to the con artist.

Does that make sense? A person can't be one dimensional. Their mind and emotions must be working together to bring them to the point where they can trust self and what they see happening in their life. Without that self-trust they will be second guessing self, which will cause them to interrupt the event and not understand what is happening.

I had finished my program and was making my way out of the room when he reached over and grabbed my arm. I stopped, turned and saw the look of pain in his eyes.

"Do you have a minute we can talk," he said in a very shaky voice.

I knew this was one of those moments in life where his desire must be a top priority. "Sure. Let's step outside where it is quiet."

We walked outside, found a quiet place and sat down. I decided this was his meeting, so I just sat there waiting for him to speak.

Realizing I was waiting on him, he looked me squarely

in the eye and said in his still shaky voice, "Can I trust you?"

"What do you mean?"

"Can I trust you? I need to talk to someone and the last two people I have talked to have taken what I told them and shared it with the people I was trying to talk to them about. Can I trust you?"

I paused, looked him squarely in the eye and said, "What do you think? Do you feel you can trust me?"

"My heart tells me I can. There is just something I felt about you when you were speaking that said you were not placed in my life by accident. I wasn't suppose to be at the convention, but at the last moment things changed and I decided to come. Maybe you are the reason I was to be here. I am so torn on the inside and don't know what to do."

"Why don't you tell me what is going on inside of you. Let's see if we can make sense out of it. If there is one thing I am good at, it is being a great set of ears. I don't always have an answer, but I can always ask the right question."

"I just don't trust people anymore. I have always been a trusting person. I would take people at their word and never question what they told me, but all that has changed."

There was this long pause as he stared off into the distance. I could feel the emotions that were racing through him. The pain I had seen in his eyes was now taking over his entire presence. Whatever was going on inside him was a major emotional point of conflict for him.

With his eyes still fixed on the distance he continued his conversation with himself that I was allowed to listen to.

"I came to this group from another network marketing company. In my former life I was one of the top income earners in the entire organization. I went there because I believed in the people. I felt they were genuine and had a strong sense of ethics. In the beginning I asked a lot of questions and they said all the right things, but I soon found out that saying the right thing doesn't always mean you will do the right thing. Your words, *Behavior Never Lies*, are what reached out and grabbed my heart. I had never heard it put that way before. I guess I wanted so much to believe these people that I didn't pay attention to what they were doing. Richard, they were speaking out of both corners of their mouth. They were good; they knew exactly what to say, and I bought it hook, line and sinker."

Again there was this long pause and he reflected on what he was talking about. As I watched his eyes, I could feel the pain turn to anger. I could see the anger creating a storm inside of him.

"They really hurt you didn't they?"

"Yes; I trusted them and they took that trust and used it against me."

"Matt, you are going to have to work through this. You can't continue to bottle all this up inside you. If you do, you will never get beyond it. It will grow, fester and destroy your ability to ever believe in people again. Do you understand if you don't dispel this anger, it just becomes baggage you take with you wherever you go? It can keep you from being successful with your network marketing business. It can make you a very old and very skeptical man. Is that how you want to live your life?"

"NO! That is why I asked if I could trust you. I understand the need to dump this. My wife has told me she sees major changes going on inside me. She told me last night I needed to do something before my anger takes over my entire life. I know she is right, but when you have trusted someone and then find they had lied to you, it hurts. I believed in these people; I brought lots of people into the organization because I trusted them. Then, they took everything I believed in and destroyed it with their behavior. Man, are you right! Behavior is where it all is. I just wish you had walked into my life a year ago."

"You would not have been ready for me. We are talking because you are ready to move on. Up until now you were not ready. You were lost in the internal battle of anger you were more interested in fighting than resolving. Now you are more interested in resolving your emotional conflict than continuing the war. Now you were ready for my presence in your life. That is why my words reached out and grabbed you."

There are a lot of Matt's out there. I hear their stories through phone calls, face-to-face visits and emails. They have been emotionally damaged because of the contradiction between the spoken word and the acted out behavior. One must not forget that the essence of who a person is, is defined by their behavior. What happens when there is the contradiction between what is said and what is done through behavior?

The first thing is <u>confusion sets in</u>. That is a guarantee. If one feels they can't trust what they are being told, they will be confused. That confusion will make them question anything that is said to them. That in turn will set loose a host of emotions for them to wrestle with. One will find self struggling with doubt, worry and a strong sense of uncertainty. They won't know who to believe or if to believe what they are being told. That will only feed the confusion and weaken any trust they have left.

Confusion creates doubts. Those doubts can crack the foundation of trust one has had. When trust is cracked, it can never be taken back to where it was. When one's heart is damaged, the result is that person trying to protect self from pain. Please understand this. *Trust that has been cracked can be repaired, but not rebuilt to its original condition.* The crack is permanent. It will always be there in the form of an emotional scar.

Confusion is a tough emotion to face. It steals one's clarity and leaves them in a world where very few things make sense. Clarity is one's mind showing them the pathway through the situation. As long as a person has clarity, things make sense, BUT take away the clarity and they will find self feeling lost and not sure what the right decision is. That will paralyze them and leave them trapped in the circle of sameness.

Contradictions will <u>open a person</u> to <u>negative emotions</u>. I don't care how positive a person is when they come face to face with the contradiction between what is said and what is delivered through behavior, they will react. Being able to trust what someone says, keeps them focused on the positive? As long as a person can trust what is being said to them, they will focus on finding and implementing what they know they need to do to improve, BUT let the contradiction happen and the trust weakens. Then, they will wrestle with negative emotions. When negative feelings set in, one's imagination weakens and their emotions increase. That is a dangerous time because it pushes them away from responding and opens them to reacting to what they feel is going on.

The contradiction will <u>narrow one's choices</u>. When one can't trust what is said to them, their mind is filled with possibilities. They are constantly seeking the next level of the journey. Yes, there are negative things going on around them, but they are focused on implementing the decisions that will

71

keep them headed toward growth and the achievement of their dream. Let confusion set in and watch as negative feelings create doubt that is stronger than their beliefs and watch what happens. All of the sudden they are not sure what to do. They are not sure who to believe. They are not sure if this is the right place for them. They slip into questioning everything they have been told. That means their choices have been narrowed. A person needs clarity and calmness to make the right decisions. Without these two they will look at the situation and this huge sense of uncertainty will take over. Now they are handcuffed with fear.

The contradiction will also <u>take the wind out of one's sails</u>. Let me go back to Matt for a moment. Listen to what he told me.

"Richard, I felt like I had no energy. I had trusted everything these people told me. I was there. I was part of the journey they were talking about and then, their real agenda came out and I realized I had been lied to. I don't mean just once. If it had only been once, I could have handled it, BUT it was over and over again. I felt like someone had stuck a pin in my party balloon and I was emotionally drained."

To achieve anything a person must have energy. The energy is what gets them through the valleys that are always part of the journey. When they are down, they can reach inside, find the energy and make it through. If that energy supply has been depleted and there is an empty lake, rather than a reservoir they can dip into, they will not be able to recapture the spirit needed to make it through.

Some people talk about this being "knocked down;" others say "their cage has been rattled;" no matter what it is called, a person's spirit is weak and they don't have the internal energy to push them through.

This plays havoc with their motivation and ability to stay focused. When these two are weak, one will find their self wrestling with the "what if" game. That is a game one cannot win.

I have watched so many who have walked away from what could have been a real opportunity for them. Their negative feelings that were the result of disappointment reached out and drained their energy. When they needed to be able to recharge, they couldn't. When they needed to be able to reach out and tap into another's energy cell, they were too skeptical. They didn't feel they could trust what they were being told.

Each of us knows our self better than anyone. If a person needed an emotional shoulder and didn't feel there was anyone they could really trust, would we think they might drop deeper into an emotional cave where they could hide?

There has to be trust to keep our sails full. There has to be those around our life that one can reach out to in order to control the confusion and walk through their moments of uncertainty.

The contradiction will also <u>reward one's negative fears</u>. All people will always live with fears; that is a fact of life, BUT fear doesn't have to be a negative. When one's fear is controlled, it feeds their calmness and clarity. If the fear stares at the wrongs one perceives is in their life, it will control them and leave them confused with what they feel they are facing.

It keeps coming back to trust. When one can trust what is being said to them, they have this sense of calmness that surrounds the situation, BUT let that feeling of trust turn to fear and they will question what is being said to them.

73

Let's go back to Matt's words for a moment —"Can I trust you?" This was not really a question. It was a reaction to where he had been. He was speaking out of his negative fear, which had made him skeptical and weakened his trust.

He was wounded and the wounds were still emotionally open. He wanted and needed to talk, but his past experience made him skeptical. That is a major avenue negative fears uses in a person's life. As long as they are skeptical, they enter situations feeling uncertain about what to do or whom they can believe. Most will not confront their skepticism; they will retreat and bury what they need to unload. The result is the strengthening of their negative fear to the point it owns them emotionally.

The contradiction between what is said and what is done will also <u>affirm one's negative fears</u>. It is interesting to watch people who have had a history of being hurt or being lied to. When it reappears in their life, it brings back all the old memories and causes them to vividly relive the old tapes. The result is moving deeper into their pattern of withdrawal and coming up with more reasons why they can't trust anyone.

Manny put it this way. "I want to trust and believe what is being said to me, but I have had so many tell me I can trust them only to be part of their ugly agenda. The last time I really worked to overcome the fear I had and I did it. I reached out and one more time trusted that someone meant what they were saying. Know what? It was the same situation all over again. They took what I told them and used it against me. It just reaffirmed the fact you can't trust anyone."

What a lonely life she was designing for herself. When one's negative fear reaches the point where they are no longer willing to trust, they are left with a very lonely existence.

Without the feeling of being able to trust, a person locks self into a world of disbelief. They look at others as the enemy; they just know if they share with them, they are going to get hurt. The result is one storing everything and making self an emotional wreck.

The contradiction between what is said and what is done will <u>destroy one's respect for another</u>. In any relationship how important is respect? I believe it is one of the most important foundational components. Respect is part of what allows one person to trust another; respect is what makes one want to listen and believe; respect allows one to stand in the presence of another and feel safe and secure. Take the respect away and what is left? The leftovers contain a huge amount of doubt, disbelief, mistrust and the feeling they have been used. When respect is taken away, one cuts a major life support that holds relationships together.

The contradiction between what is said and what is done will <u>involve the feeling a person has been used</u>. So many times I have heard the same words I heard from Matt, "They used me!" It is a strange feeling to feel one has been part of another's hidden agenda. It is a sinking feeling to find out they were used.

Here one puts their feelings on the line, trust what they are told and then, find self sucked into a situation they didn't anticipate. In the beginning they didn't pay close attention to the person's behavior. They just trusted the person, so they let the behavior slide. Sure they noticed some inconsistencies, but because they trusted what they were told and the person who said it, they just dropped it as not important.

Then, a situation happens and they are awakened to the contradiction between what they have been told and the behavior. Their eyes are now wide open and their ears are tuned into what is being said. The more they listen the more aware they become of what is really happening. It is no longer just about what they are being told; it is about the contradiction between what they have been told and what is being done.

They can't believe they got sucked in. How could they have been that stupid? How could they not have seen what was really going on?

Trust is participation without questions. That is a good and a bad thing. Yes, one needs to trust, but no, they don't need to trust with their blinders on. Anytime one just blindly trust they are setting self up for disappointment.

Trust needs to be supported with behavior. It is not the words that say one can trust a person; it is their behavior.

Now, I am not saying enter everything as a skeptic, but I am saying approach everything with an awareness of their behavior. Don't just listen; listen and watch. When what one is hearing is not supported by the behavior, stop and question what is happening. If one doesn't, they are going to wake up feeling used and abused.

The contradiction between what is said and what is done will <u>create a crossroads where a decision will have to be made</u>. This is major.

Trust is only solid when the spoken word and behavior are in sync. As long as that is what one is seeing, they can move forward and not worry about conflict, confusion or concentration. When trust is bruised or torn through contradiction, they find self living in a world of worry, doubt and uncertainty. Put these three together and watch the internal conflict it creates.

No longer will a person accept what they hear on

pure face value. No longer will they simply take what is said without this inner feeling of whether they can trust it or not. One finds self dealing with questions they can't answer; they find self wrestling with emotions that take them in a direction they are not comfortable with. The lack of trust surrounds them with all these emotions they aren't used to wrestling with. Now, they stand at a crossroad and aren't sure what to do. They want to believe, but the cracked foundation makes it challenging for them to feel they are standing on solid ground.

Bert and Crystal are two of the finest people a person will ever meet. They live in a world where right is right and wrong is wrong. They have a strong spiritual foundation that holds their lives together.

Recently, Bert had his world rocked. For 30 years he has worked at a CPA firm he helped build. For 30 years he poured his heart and soul into helping the other partners build the Practice to one of the most respected in the area. For 30 years he committed himself to providing the highest quality of service to his customers that was possible. For 30 years he saw the Practice as something he could believe in and go to work each day without questioning how the Practice was going to be run.

Recently the Practice merged with another CPA firm. On the surface it looked like a good marriage. There seemed to be a shared agenda and they were all in sync with the mission of taking care of their customers. Once the merger was completed, the new Managing Partner started slowly introducing his personal agenda, which was not at all what had been stated in the pre-merger talks. Now, the shift was from taking care of the customer to taking care of the bottom line. It became another institution that was all about making money.

For years the Senior Partners had handed business down to the Junior Partners. This was done to prepare them for the future and to allow the Senior Partners to spend more time with the top clients.

Now, the Senior Partners were being questioned about their hours. What had been the agenda was now the confusion. Bert, like others, found himself having to justify what he had been told was his role. He was involved in several groups outside the Practice that created visibility for the Practice and helped to strengthen their reputation within the business community. For years this was a part of what the Senior Partners were to be doing. Now, the new power questioned whether this was the proper use of time.

Now, add to this a group of Junior Partners from Generation X. The majority of this Generation X group thought they were paid too little and the Senior Partners were paid too much. It didn't matter the years the Senior Partners had put into building the Practice to where it was today. It didn't matter all the hours that had been invested in building accounts to where they were now. All that seemed to matter to this group of Junior Partners was that they weren't being paid enough and the Senior Partners were being paid way too much.

Practice compensation was controlled by a compensation committee, which is elected by all the Partners. Since the Junior Partners out numbered the Senior Partners, it was stacked with those Junior Partners who felt they weren't paid enough.

As they reviewed each of the Senior Partner's compensation, they determined it was too much and needed to be refigured with compensation being more equally distributed among all the partners. It didn't matter how long one had been there; it didn't matter the years of building that had been spent building the volume of Practice business. All that mattered was that they wanted more money.

Bert was told his compensation was going be reduced by 38%. The reason he was given was that most of his book of business was now being done by others. Since he was no longer generating the volume he once had, there needed to be an adjustment to his income.

Put yourself in Bert's place. How would you feel? Thirty years you have given your blood, your time and your energy to building a very successful Practice only to have a group of people (who didn't want to pay the price, but thought they should share in the results) take control of your future.

How would any person respond when told, "You can rebuild your compensation by going out and generating new business." But there was no guarantee that this group of money hungry, non-accountable people wouldn't turn around and do this to you all over again. Would anyone in their right mind trust what they were being told?

Bert was told he could go in front of the compensation committee and sell them on the fact he was worth his compensation and it shouldn't be changed. He and I talked about how to approach the committee. He knew what they were going to throw at him as their justification for their actions.

I told Bert, "Let's turn the table on them. Everything they are using as their reason for readjusting your compensation has not been substituted. It is all conjecture. Let's go into the meeting and interview them."

The more he thought about it the more he realized the wisdom in doing that. No one was holding them accountable for their behavior; no one was challenging their right to do what they were doing.

79

Prior to the meeting, Bert visited with all the people they had used as their justification for their decision. As he talked to them, he got a different story from what he had been told.

In the meeting each time they bought up one of their reasons, Bert countered with facts. It didn't take long for them to realize their behavior was being confronted. Soon, there was nothing but silence. Bert felt good about the meeting, but those on the committee were angered by his questions.

Bert learned there was some serious discussion after he left, but they had decided to reduce his compensation by 38%. Yes, they said they wanted him to stay. They wanted him to know he was valuable to the future of the Practice. They knew he could generate new business and earn back a part of his lost compensation.

Bert felt so devalued. Thirty years of his life being tossed aside because he had worked to make the Practice successful.

His words to me were, "Richard, I heard you say in one of your presentations *never stay anywhere where your presence is not appreciated.* You also told me I would know when it was time to move on with my life. When I see what they have done and how much their behavior says I don't matter, I know it is now time for me to move on."

There was a great amount of sadness in his voice as he continued, "I was hoping it wouldn't come to this, but what am I suppose to do. I don't trust them; I don't respect who they are or what they are doing. I think their behavior is unethical. When I put all that together, they have left me no option."

There was a long pause as he gathered himself. "I am standing at that crossroad you keep talking about. If I just suck it up and give in, I become their hostage. If I just accept what they want me to accept, I have to weaken my principles and become like them. I am not willing to do that. I am a person of worth! I am a person of value! I can make a difference! It will just not be where I thought it would be."

How many times is this picture being painted in corporate America today? How many people are being tossed aside because others want to benefit from their years of effort and not have to pay the price of work, sacrifice and accountability? They have been told for years that they matter; they have worked for years to build the company through their effort, BUT then, there is a merger or a new look at the top and all that was and all those great things that were said are no longer true. The emphasis now shifts from people to profit. The new regime is willing to sacrifice the people whose efforts have brought the company to the place where it is profitable. Those who see the bottom line as more important than the people who have made that bottom line possible are willing to just toss them aside and justify it with the need to cut cost.

Know what I find interesting about all of this. Those who control the future of others and announce the need to cut the bottom line still pay themselves their huge salaries. They are willing to sacrifice the lives of others while lining their pockets with the profits. I wish they would give me solid reasons for their behavior.

The irony in all this is many who have been given their walking papers are being hired back as consultants and being paid more than they were making as an employee.

Only when they are no longer there, is their real value understood. Many who are kept don't have the work ethic of those who have been dismissed, nor the desire to really want to perform. They want to come to work, do their thing their way, collect their check and go home. They don't bring the commitment; they don't bring the professionalism; they are actually costing the company profit with their lack of quality presence. Then, companies wonder why the consumer is upset with their products, their service, their treatment of them. They don't want to face their behavior and the repercussion it has created. Their behavior has taken the consumer to a crossroads where they will make a decision. Their product and/or service may be good, but the behavior of their people is not acceptable and the consumer is unwilling to tolerate the treatment.

It is challenging for any company to maintain a high level of quality, trust or respect when what those at the top are saying is being contradicted by what they are doing through behavior.

The contradiction between words and behavior will allow pain to linger for years. Pain is more than an event that inflicted hurt; it is an internal scar that always has a presence.

I have said for years as much as we preach and teach forgive and forget, it is a test most people can't pass. It is not as challenging to forgive, IF the person being forgiven doesn't continue to repeat the behavior they are being forgiven for. If their behavior improves and doesn't constantly repeat itself, there is a healing that takes place over a period of time. BUT if one forgives and the behavior continues, the spirit of forgiveness turns to anger, which will accelerate to hate. Once it reaches hate, it becomes a permanent scar.

Alicia put it this way to me. "I have tolerated his behavior for twelve years. At first I was willing to forgive and just accept it as his immaturity, but it has been twelve years and it is still the same crap. He keeps telling me I'm sorry; I am working on myself, but after twelve years you would have thought he would have made some improvements. I can't forgive him anymore; no, the truth is I don't want to forgive him anymore. I am tired of his lies and his words that never happen. I just want him out of my life."

Those were tough words, but they were the result of the continued contradiction between words of promise and behavior of sameness.

Maggie put it this way. "I know the Bible teaches that I should forgive seven times seventy, but what is his responsibility? I forgive and he continues, and this has been his pattern for years. I am tired of forgiving. How can you forgive and forget when it is the same behavior over and over? I don't think God expects me to forgive when there is no repentance on his part."

Pain is a constant reminder of the infliction that behavior has created. Pain is always present; it doesn't go away just because a person asked for forgiveness and tells the other person they are sorry and won't do it again. Pain is a scar that constantly reminds them of why it is present.

Now, don't read more into this than I am writing. Yes, one should forgive, BUT only if the behavior that inflicted the pain isn't constantly repeated. Yes, one should forgive and work through the hurt in order to forget the depth of the pain. Understand, everyone is human and as a human, pain will always have residue in one's life. Those scars that were created by behavior are always present and can reopen at any time. It takes a lot of work and the consistency of improved behavior to keep them from reopening and bringing back the feelings that created them in the first place.

Forgiveness is possible! Forgetting is challenging!

Moving on after emotional pain has been inflicted is a lot of work. Rebuilding a strong commitment to making today a new experience takes a lot of patient consistent persistency. If one is working on rebuilding and the other is simply playing a game by using the right words, then forgiveness shouldn't be the mission and without that forgetting will not be possible.

Words are what one hears; behavior is what they see. Forgiving and forgetting takes both of these working together, which allows one to overcome the pain through the proof of behavior.

Put together all we have talked about in the previous pages about what happens when the contradiction between words and behavior come together, it creates a very disappointing picture. Yet, the real damage is done as these come together and create the last three of our understandings about the contradictions between words and actions. In my working with human behavior these three become the most dangerous. All we have talked about in the previous pages are realistic, but not as internally damaging as these last three. These last three are where the lingering effects will happen. Pay close attention to these.

The contradiction between what is said and behavior will <u>shatter the idealism one has lived with</u>. People are not born as skeptics; I really believe the basic nature of any human is to trust. One has to learn how to be skeptical; they have to learn how to look for the bad; they have to learn to not believe.

Ray put it this way. "In the beginning, I believed everything she told me. Even when I wasn't sure, my feelings for her made me give her the benefit of the doubt. I just knew she was different; I just knew for the first time I had found someone that I could put my total trust in and not be disappointed. BUT, over a period of time I found myself no longer willing to give her that benefit of doubt. There were just too many inconsistencies. It was like every time she disappointed me a little part of me died. Finally, I had to admit I was being a fool."

Ray wasn't being a fool! He was just like 99% of people. They have this idealistic spirit that wants to believe the best about another person. They want to believe they are who they say they are. In that space and time they don't look for the inconsistencies. In that venue they overlook those things, BUT when the inconsistencies have a greater presence than the times of consistencies, they soon slow down and start paying attention to the contradictions between their spoken word and behavior.

At some point the person wakes up and their little world of idealism comes crashing down around them. What happens? They find self frustrated, disappointed, drained, filled with disbelief and creating an outer emotional wall around self. They keep asking self, "How could I have been that dumb?" They beat self down with thoughts like, "I must not be a very deserving person to have someone do this to me." They start making self responsible for what has happened.

Reality is the person was just living in their idealistic world where their desire to trust was stronger than their mental sight. There is nothing wrong with that. That is what one has to hear. If a person enters every aspect of their life filled with doubt and skepticism, they would never develop any relationships. They would live in a cave and never come out or let anyone come in.

There has to be the spirit of belief. There has to be the internal desire to trust. When things go wrong, it is not saying one is a bad person. Being conned is not a sign that one is a bad person; it is just telling them, they have met someone who was able to play with their desire to believe. Don't throw that away! Learn from the experience and move forward. There are people out there one can believe in; there are people out there one can trust. Don't make self the enemy because you want to believe!

This feeds right into the second of these three key feelings that happen when the spoken word is contradicted by behavior. The contradiction will <u>offset what one has been</u>. There is so much danger here. Time and time again I have watched people in personal relationships, work situations, and families go through a major personality shift because of an experience that attacked whom they saw themselves as.

Because most people's foundation of self worth is not solid, they tend to stare at the worst of the event, rather than slowing down and seeking the lesson. If one doesn't find the lesson that is contained in the event, they will repeat it over and over.

This is the critical point of understanding. The repeating of negative events in any life is the result of not finding the lesson that takes a person beyond it. If all they see is the pain, the damage, the wrong, the negative aspects, they will repeat this event. In fact they will repeat it over and over until they slow down and understand why this continues to happen to them. Fact is if they never gain the understanding, they will never get beyond it.

Rita is one of the best examples I know. For years I had the same conversation with her. Each time I saw her I would get an updated chapter of the same story she had been writing for years with her life. Oh, the characters had a different name, but the story was always the same.

Each time I talked to her I got the same question, "Richard, why am I still here? Why am I still dealing with the same stuff I have been dealing with for years?

Each time I would ask her the same question, "Rita, what are you doing to make sure you won't repeat this all over again? What have you learned from all this?"

"I guess I am just a person who isn't meant to be happy," was her standard reply.

"Rita, all of us are designed to be happy. Happiness is a choice you make and then act out with behavior. Lots of people talk about wanting to be happy in their life, but continue to do the same things that made them unhappy in their past. Their repetitive behavior is a sure sign they don't really want to be happy. If they really wanted to be happy, they would slow down, look at what is happening to their life and then make the necessary improvements. The lessons are always present; they just choose to look at the wrong, rather than seek out the lesson."

There was this long pause with a look of confusion on her face. "If that is true, why do they do that?"

I waited a couple of seconds before I answered her. I wanted to make sure she was mentally and emotionally present.

"Rita, they do it for the same reason you do it. They talk about wanting to get better, about having their life improve, but the truth is they really don't want it."

I stopped to let her absorb what I had just said. The look on her face told me she didn't like the answer.

The look on her face turned to an expression of anger. "Are you telling me I want to live my life this way?"

"That is exactly what I am telling you. You are because you choose to be. You can move beyond this situation any time you want to. You are still here because this is where you have chosen to be."

"How can you say that to me! You know how angry all this makes me. You know how many times I have told you I want to get out of this emotional trap."

"Exactly! That is what I am talking about. We have had this same conversation for several months and look at where you are. How many times have I told you this is all about the choices you are making? How many times have I said that to you?"

There was silence. She didn't know what to say. Down deep inside she knew I was right. She really loved the pain; she stayed at this place because it granted her attention and pity. When people had had enough of her story, they would just walk away. She would blame them for not really being her friend and walk out and find another person to use.

Rita had not always been this way. There was a time when she was one of the most positive and upbeat people one could have known. Then, her life got turned upside down and rather than facing the situation and moving through it, she decided to sit down and stay in her life of pain and anger. One would have wanted to feel sorry for her, but if they did, they would have been supporting her behavior. Supporting that behavior would only have fed it and given her permission to stay there longer.

She is like so many walking around in society today. They once were a person who lived, but allowed an upside down situation to offset who they were. The pain their life was handed became their reason for existing. As much as they talked about wanting their life to be better, as much as they talked about wanting to get beyond the situations in their life, the truth is they want to remain where they are.

Study their behavior and get the real message of their life. Study their behavior and see their need for pity and attention. As long as that is whom they want to be, that is who they will remain being. It is not a matter of what they can or can't do about their life; it is all about whom they want to be in their life.

Each day people choose to either face their life with truth and honesty, or to deny their life what it was meant to be. If one chooses to deny, they off-set the good that is always present just waiting for them to see, experience and accept it.

Put these two together and one gets the final aspect of this dangerous trio. The last is the most important. When there is a contradiction between what one says and what they do, the result is one no longer trusting self. How important is self trust? How strong a component is self trust to one's journey of life? What happens when one no longer trusts self? How does that affect their behavior?

These are not just questions; they are revealing thoughts that really help a person understand their behavior. I have found much of the contradiction between what one says and what they do is the result of a weakened foundation of self trust.

Most know how to talk a good story; many have read the books, listened to the tapes, been to the programs, mastered the lingo, BUT are still wrestling with behavior that keeps their life upside down.

Let me introduce a few I have met who illustrate this point.

Peter has a room filled with tapes and CD's from programs he has attended, yet he is still wrestling with a life that is less than fulfilling. When I pushed him, it all came down to his lack of self trust. He talks everyday about what he is going to do, but has yet to implement the consistency of behavior to make it a reality. He makes it through the day by talking about what he plans on doing. The bottom line is he just doesn't have the self trust to implement the behavior he knows is right.

Dorothy is talented, has the desire, but is held hostage by her fear of making it on her own. She knows what she needs to do; she can sit there and tell a person step by step what needs to happen in her life, BUT her fear of doing it on her own keeps her locked into a world of behavior that weakens her talents and each day strengthens her excuses with her behavior. Her behavior will keep her trapped in a world that is exhausting her life. The truth is she just doesn't trust herself!

Nickie has read all the books; she has been to the psychologist and knows all the buzzwords. She can quote the symptoms and the cures, BUT today she is wrestling with the same challenges that took her to the counselors in the first place. One can sit with her and she is great at diagnosing herself, BUT she has yet to implement any of this in her behavior. The truth is she just doesn't have the self trust to step into what she sees as a world of uncertainty. As painful as today is to her, it is more secure than the world that lies on the other side of her repetitive behavior.

Grant is "Mr. Personality." Take him anywhere and he is the life of the party. Everyone likes Grant, but few believe anything he tells them. He exists through his personality, BUT now he has hit a crossroads where his personality cannot take him any further. There is a great future in front of him, but to get there, he has to face his insecurity and step into a world where he will have to trust himself. Since that has not been his behavior for 40+ years, it is much easier for him to justify finding a new direction for his life, rather than face the fact he is a hostage trapped in a world where he hides from his lack of self trust. He will simply turn, walk away and find another place where he can be "Mr. Personality." He will stay there until he reaches the same place where his behavior will become his enemy; then, he will again have to either face his lack of self trust or run away again.

None of these people are isolated stories. They are real people who live each day fearing who they are. They are real people who lack the most important foundation in life — self trust.

I will say it again and again and again. Study the behavior of any person and it gives the full definition of whom they see themselves as. Their behavior is the essence of what they think, what they know, what they want for their life and what they fear. The connecting point for all of this is self trust.

Words are what a person speaks; behavior is who they are. *Behavior Never Lies*. One can talk all they want, but until their words and behavior are in sync, they will live in this ugly circle that each day brings them back to the same point where they started. When one can't see any exit out of this circle, it will steal their spirit, color their life with a black cloud and send them to their grave never knowing what they could have accomplished in their life. That is not living; that is walking through life existing in a world filled with all the excuses, all the blame and everyday justifying where they are with what has gone wrong in their life. That is not living! That is existing in a world where happiness, personal fulfillment and freedom are simply words they don't get to experience. Only when a person's words and behavior are working together can they experience what their life was meant to be. The real definition of their life is seen in their behavior; that is who they really are; their behavior will define what they believe and define what they can and will become in their life.

Chapter 5

# Living In Sync!

*Without balance there is confusion in all areas
of your life.*

Life is about being honest with self. It begins by being able to look in one's mirror of life and see whom they really are, not who they talk about becoming.

Life is about a person believing in self. Sure, there are going to be moments of doubt, but if one truly believes in self, they will take those moments of doubt and turn them into learning points that will make them personally stronger.

Life is about trusting self. This is such a critical part of a person's life journey. They are who they see their self being. The person one sees is created by how much they believe in self; that belief is controlled by whether they trust or distrust self.

Life is about being in sync. It is about one working with, not against self. Their ability to work from within in order to keep their life moving at a pace they can manage is the result of them being honest, believing in self and trusting in who they are.

When one is in sync, their words and behavior will be aligned to create a straight line between where they are and where they are going. That line will be controlled and strengthened by their behavior.

Is the message clear? Are those three little words finally sinking in? There is power to those three little words, *Behavior Never Lies!*

A person really is whom they act out, not whom they say they are. When there is a contradiction between the spoken word and the acted out behavior, there is total confusion. A person is confused because they know the lie they are living. Those around their life are confused because they see the contradictions. It becomes a world where one is trapped in their exhausting Circle of Sameness. It becomes a world where they can't see any way out; it becomes a world where they just want to throw up their hands and give up; it becomes a world where they exist and not live; it becomes a world where they can't find the meaning of their life. It becomes a self-defeating life!

Behavior Never Lies! Are we tired? I mean really tired, of not living? Are we ready, and I mean really ready, to have the life that brings happiness, personal fulfillment and personal freedom?

The solution is simple, but challenging. It can be done, but not without a lot of personal discovery and behavioral redesigning. It doesn't just happen; it is a process that takes consistent persistency based on persistent consistency. If one wants it and I mean really wants it, it can be theirs.

There are eight principles one will have to master. Now, I am not talking about just accepting; there are eight principles one will have to master. They will not be easy; they will challenge any person and they will find self wrestling with their meaning to their life. They will find self not wanting to do what they know they need to do. One can't accept some parts and reject the others. This is a process that requires all or nothing. It is a process that has one order to it. If one decides they don't like one step and avoids it, the process won't work. Like anything there is an order that must be followed.

Steve called me three days after we had the discussed the war he was fighting between the "Old" and "New" Steve. When I picked up the phone I heard, "You know I don't always take everything you say as being 100% correct?"

"I know you Steve. I know you live in your own Stevie world and don't always really listen to everything I say. I have watched you tune out and then come back when the conversation contains something you want to hear."

"You're right," he said. "I have always been one who seems to cut and paste conversations. For instance, you remember when we were talking the other day about this war you said I was fighting?"

"Yes."

"I really didn't believe that stuff about there being a battle internally between an "Old" and a "New" me. I listened to what you said, but sort of wrote it off."

"If you wrote it off, why are we having this discussion?"

"One thing you did say was the battle between the "Old" and the "New" me was going to increase. Well, it has. I have never felt so frustrated, so angry, so uncertain about what to do as I am right now. There is so much conflict inside me. I have to be honest with you. It is wearing me down."

There was a long pause and I knew he was wrestling with all the emotions that were going on inside him.

"Richard, I can't handle this alone. I have never been a person to ask for help. I have always felt I was strong enough to get through everything on my own, BUT this is one time I can't do this by myself. This is so hard for me to say, but I need your help."

"Steve, all of us go through times when we need to reach out. What do you see as your #1 challenge?"

"My inconsistency! I am a great talker, but then I don't do anything. I will never forget when I first heard you say *Behavior Never Lies*. Every time I find myself saying something I know I am not going to do, I hear those words. Each time I start something and then push it aside, those words play in my mind. I have got to get my life in sync. I have to say what I mean and mean what I say. I have been so inconsistent people don't take me seriously anymore. I don't want to be this way. Will you help me?"

Steve is not alone in his struggle. Most people struggle with the contradiction between what they say and what they do. Most live creating their own internal conflict. One can't live out of sync without conflict; one can't have contradictions without having confusion. The great news is a person doesn't have to live with the contradictions. They don't have to get lost in the confusion the contradictions create. They can be in sync and move their life forward with calmness and clarity. The secret is understanding and implementing the process to achieve this. There are eight steps to balancing one's words and behavior.

Now, these eight steps are not a magical formula; there are no magical formulas. This process is about a person standing tall within their self and making self responsible for the design of their life. It is no longer allowing self to blame others for what they aren't; it is about a person no longer using reasons to define what is or is not happening in their life; it is a person moving beyond justifying their life. It is the realization that a person *is perfectly designed to achieve what they are achieving.*

That is it in a nutshell; a person is because they choose to be, not because they have to be. They are living their design and that means they are the only one who can change that design. They are the only one who can control their behavior and bring it into sync with what they say. There are eight steps to making this happen.

**Step 1 — Believing In You:** It all has to start here. If a person doesn't believe in who they are, the doubt and uncertainty this creates will feed their inner war and keep conflict as a central part of their life.

**Step 2 — Expanding Your Horizon:** If the life one is living is the same life they have been living, the struggles they are having will be the same they have been having. That means they are trapped and controlled by their Circle of Sameness. The result will be a life that is designed to repeat, not improve.

**Step 3 — Holding Yourself Accountable:** This is where the process begins to turn very personal. Too many have had their world of excuses, reasons and justifications validated by the others in their life who won't confront their behavior. As long as a person doesn't have to be accountable for their behavior, they won't!

**Step 4 — Addressing Your Inconsistencies:** An inconsistency is a contradiction. It is the visual definition of what a person really feels. One can say what they want with their words, but their behavior is the truth. When the visual contradicts the spoken, there are inconsistencies.

**Step 5 — Very Carefully Align Yourself With The Right People:** A person's circle of people around their life is another definition of who one is and what they want to be. Those who want to improve their life surround their life with people who are challenging self and the others who are in their life. Those who want to stay the same surround their life with people who give them permission to stay where they are. Look at the people one has in their life and there is a picture of whom they are.

**Step 6 — Increase Your Awareness**: A person has to be aware of what is happening in their life. They can't live with blinders on; they can't plead ignorance; they can't use reasons and excuses to justify their life.

**Step 7 — Operate Your Life At A Manageable Pace**: Pace is so important to balancing one's life. If one's pace is managing them, their life is out of control. That means no matter how hard they work to create consistency it will become a war they can't win.

**Step 8 — Refusing To Go Backward**: This is the commitment. This is the statement of strength. The challenge for everyone is the consistent persistency to remain persistently consistent. That is the war! It is easy to make the commitment to improve one's behavior; those statements happen every day. The real challenge is to maintain the behaviors of improvement. For most it is easier to talk about their needs. They are serious about what they are talking about; they know what they need to do, but when it comes to implementing, the war begins.

These eight steps are a process; they are not something one can casually play with. For a person to bring their life in sync where their words and behavior are saying the same thing takes an awareness to what they are doing, the honesty to face their behavior and the strength to maintain the journey in spite of all their life is handed.

These eight steps become a person's battle plan. The inner war a person fights each day is not a casual scrimmage; it is an all out war being fought for control of one's life. There is always a winner and the winner gets control of that life. How is the winner determined? Just look at the behavior of the person.

Remember, *Behavior Never Lies!*

These next eight chapters create guidelines that will provide one with the understandings necessary to find the pathway through the crossroads and intersections of confusion that they will face throughout their life. Don't just look at these eight steps as thoughts; see them for what they are; these eight steps offers one the calmness and clarity necessary to balance what they say with what they do.

Find the truth in those three words, *Behavior Never Lies!*

Chapter 6

# I'm Worth Believing In!

## Step One: Believing In You

*Without a strong foundation of self belief a person will constantly be struggling with doubt, worry and a sense of uncertainty.*

The process starts with you *believing in you*. It has to start here. Without a strong foundation of inner belief, a person's entire life is shrouded in doubt. Doubt keeps them staring at whom they aren't, not who they could be. As long as that is the picture they have of self, they will live in a world filled with problems and based in negative beliefs. When these two are acted out, they create behaviors that hold a person hostage, not behaviors that set them free.

When I met Tonya, she was a wreck. She had driven eight hours to attend my program in Minneapolis. One of her friends had seen me months before and told her, "You need to go listen to this guy."

At this point in her life she was desperate. Her business life was in shambles; her love life was a vacant room and she sure didn't want to spend any time with herself.

One couldn't miss her in the seminar room. She was on the front row and every time I said something that smacked her she would groan out loud. My words created so much personal pain within her she moaned out loud. I noticed at the conclusion of the program she didn't move. When I came back to pack up, she was still sitting there. The look on her face told me she was frozen. She wanted to move, but couldn't.

I walked over, sat down and just looked at her. Finally, she turned to me and in a voice filled with pain and torment said, "I don't like me. I don't think I have ever liked me. If I don't like me, how can I believe in me?"

"You can't! Until you like who you are you won't trust yourself. If you don't trust yourself, you can't believe in yourself."

That started a journey of us working together. The journey was designed to understand and rewrite the script she had for her life. Everyone has a script. It is that script that creates their feelings, which they then translate into behavior. Many people don't understand the power of those scripts. They are not just words that have created the script one lives. They are implants that become imbedded in one's personal opinions about self. They create feelings a person accepts as truth and acts out through their behavior. Too many people never challenge their internal program. They just accept it and spend their life proving it through their behavior. Truth is many of these scripts are lies; they are not who the person is; these scripts create what others have programmed them to be. Because of who these programmers are, most people don't challenge what they have said. They just accept it as truth and live to fulfill their program. They have become their creation, not the original God intended them to be. They have given up their individuality.

That was Tonya. She had been programmed by her mother to believe she was not intelligent, not pretty and would always live a life filled with problems and pain. Know what? That is exactly who she became. She was what her mother had been programming her to be.

I will never forget the day I handed her a mirror and asked her, "Tell me what you see?"

She stared for a few seconds at her image in the mirror and just started crying. "I don't see anyone. I just see this dark image I don't like."

"Why? Why a dark image?"

"Because I don't want to see that person. I don't like her. She is not a good person."

In a short time we figured out that was one of the programs her mother had instilled in her. Her mother had daily programmed her with the thoughts, "You are stupid; you are a very ugly girl; no one is ever going to want you; you will always be lonely and unhappy."

Those programs had formed the foundation of personal beliefs Tonya had about Tonya. She had accepted them as truth and based her personal definition of who she was around them.

Talk about a challenge. Here was a beautiful lady who lived in a world of darkness when it came to understanding herself. Those programs could not be erased; they had to be challenged. Those programs could not be ignored; they had to be confronted. I would watch her make progress and then, her mother would call. The next time she would show up and all the work we had done would be in shambles. It took a few months to get her to realize her mother didn't want her to get better.

At a session I asked her, "Tonya, have you told your mother we are working together?"

"Yes! She wanted to know where these foolish ideas I was sharing with her were coming from. I told her you and I were working together and she got angry. I mean really angry. She was screaming at me on the phone. She made me promise I would call her after each of our sessions."

"Have you called her?"

"Yes."

"When you call her, what does she say?"

"She wants to know what we talked about. When I tell her, she tells me what is wrong with what you are saying."

"How does that make you feel?"

"I am really confused. When we talk, I feel good. Then, I call her and she tells me you are just using me."

"How am I supposed to be using you?"

"You are just filling my head with psycho babble and none of it means anything."

"Tonya, do you understand your mother is your enemy?"

"What do you mean?"

"She doesn't want you to get better. She doesn't want you to find out who you really are and gain a sense of who you can become. If that happens, she loses control over your life. You are her pawn in the game she is playing with your life. She wants you to remain under her control. Tonya, if this is going to work, you have to stop talking to her. You have to remove her from your life. I know that is not what you want to hear, but it is the step you have to take if you are to move forward. Can you do that?"

That thought created a look of terror I could see in her eyes. I knew we had reached our first major wall of resistance. She knew I was right, but couldn't see herself without having her mother in her life. After all, her mother had written the script she was living; that was all she knew and she didn't trust herself enough to believe she could write her own script. She didn't believe in herself enough to see a life where she stood on her own two feet.

She would not talk to her mother for a while. That would cause her mother to show up at her house and make her talk to her. Each time that happened Tonya would take a step backward. We would talk about her mother's intentions. We would talk about *all behavior has an agenda*. We would talk about her mother's agenda of keeping Tonya as her prisoner. The conversation would give her the courage to resist the pressure and guilt her mother kept attacking her with.

It took us almost two years to undo the programming her mother had done to her. There were fears we had to work through; there were huge moments of doubt that almost derailed us; they were the constant interferences from her mother that we had to pause and confront. At one point I had to stop and confront her mother. It was a tense moment, but she knew I was not going to let her continue to hold her daughter hostage through her programming. That was a phone call I told Tonya either she made or I would make it. I was the one who made it and her mother was not a nice person to talk to. She tried every way to get me to back down, to turn Tonya loose, but I kept telling her in many different voice tones that her days of emotionally owning Tonya were over.

The end result was worth celebrating. Tonya really pushed herself; yes, she wanted to run away, but she stuck to the process. Yes, she had moments when she was terrified, but she slowed down and faced her fears. I was and am so proud of her.

Today, she runs her own company. During our time together, she established three major dreams for her life. She has achieved two of them and the third one is almost complete.

How important is it for a person to believe in self? In any journey, it is everything. Without a strong foundation of self-worth, a person will live with a level of personal disbelief that will keep them sabotaging their life.

For Tonya, just like it would be for any person who is really wanting to challenge their life and see how high they can soar, the starting point has to be seeking, finding and celebrating the good in their life. They have to believe that their life is about them being a person who deserves the positives that are an everyday part of life. I have always taught *you don't become what you go searching for; you become what you believe you are.* There have been many who have disagreed with that teaching, but those who have accepted it as part of their growth process have proven it correct.

Improving one's life demands a strong foundation of self worth. Self confidence, self esteem and self assurance will only be moments that lack continuation without a strong foundation of self worth. It is from the inner belief of personal value that a person creates a solid foundation of personal beliefs that don't crack when life's moments of doubt and uncertainty come rushing at them. When one really believes in self, they will be surrounded by a wall of positive beliefs that repel the negative attacks.

The challenge for most people lies in the origin of these negative tapes. Most of these misleading tapes come from our childhood; they come from someone programming a person with their agenda. At this point in life a person is not mature enough to understand what is happening. The result is an acceptance of what they are told, not challenging the intent that goes with the programming. After all, parents love their children with a pure love and would never do anything to hurt them. Because of a child's strong need for attention and approval, they are willing to take the words of parents, relatives and friends as truth. At this point in their life they don't understand some people don't love them and their intention is not to help, but control them. When they finally realize what has happened, they have already implemented their beliefs about these teachings into their life.

Like Tonya, they have to be willing to face the design of their life, confront the emotional tapes they have been listening to and redesign their picture of self. As simple as that sounds, most people know they need to do it, but lack the inner strength to see the process through.

Do you trust yourself? Do you believe you deserve good in your life? Do you believe in you? The answer to that question is not in your words, but seen in your behavior.

Remember, *Behavior Never Lies.*

**PRINCIPLES FOR LEARNING TO BELIEVE IN YOURSELF**

1. Be an original, not an actor in someone else's play.

2. Build your foundation of self worth; find the good and build on it each day.

3. Overcome the fear of facing the old negative tapes you have been programmed with.

4. Understand most of your behavior is controlled by scripts you live out each day; if the script is a lie, edit it.

5. End each day reviewing what went right that day.

6. Keep a journal filled with your successes.

7. Don't hangout with people who don't believe in you.

8. Make self improvement a daily part of your journey.

9. Don't sit at a table that is negative; feast on the positive parts of your life.

10. Study your behavior; it is the real essence of who you are.

Chapter 7

# Seeing Beyond The Moment

## Step Two: Expanding Your Horizon

*When yesterday is what is creating your picture of today, you will find yourself repeating the things you have promised you wouldn't continue to do.*

The second step in this process of balancing words with behavior requires a person to *expand their horizon*. Just as important as it is for a person to believe in self, it is a person daily seeking the correct pathway for their life.

Confusion is strengthened when one is traveling in circles, rather than in a direct line. Now, that direct line may not be a straight line, but it is the line without detours. The challenge is most people can't see the direct path because they are too busy trying to find their way through the maze they have created for themselves.

The challenge is for them to find their pathway through the confusion they have brought into their life; one has to be able to see where they want their journey to take them. When I write a book, I always write the last chapter first. Why do I do that? I want to have a clear picture in my mind of where I want to end up. Granted, many times when I get to the last chapter, I rewrite it, BUT if I hadn't had a plan about where I was going, I would have not been able to pause, refocus on where I was going and continue to move forward. The last chapter is a big part of my pathway to the beginning.

The challenge many people face is their pace. One of the emotional tools confusion uses is creating a pace a person can't mange. The faster they are moving the less calmness they have. The faster they are moving the more snap decisions they make. That means they aren't thinking; they jump in without knowing what they are jumping into. That means they don't respond; they react. That means they are always working against what they have said they are striving to achieve. Do that long enough and there will be exhaustion, being worn out and in many cases just simply giving up and settling. That just expands the circle of sameness they are existing in.

Pace is tied to believing in self. The steps in this process are not independent of each other. They work together to strengthen one from the inside out. Believing in self is a must to slowing down. The greater the foundation of self worth, the easier it is for a person to mentally and emotionally slow down and focus on what is really happening.

When one is moving at a mental and emotional pace they can't manage, they can't see the correct turns. They will race by and find self further from where they thought they were going. The result is a series of wrong turns, which create detours that steals one's energy.

Detours cannot replenish. They can only steal one's personal energy. The longer a person travels the road of detours the less mental, emotional and physical energy they have to make a course correction.

This was Leslie. Growing up she had always had a fascination with acting. In middle school, high school and college she was in every play. She always had the leading role and in her mind saw acting as her future. The challenge was her mother. Her mother would always tell her, "Leslie, it's great you love acting, but honey, you can't make a living doing that. You need to get a real career. One that will take care of you, not one that you just play at."

The relationship between Leslie and her mother was critically important to her. Her dad had died when she was five and her mother had never remarried. Leslie was an only child and had become her mother's substitute for her husband. Leslie had no life of her own; her mother planned her life for her. Any time there was something Leslie wanted to do that her mother didn't agree with there were the weapons of guilt, criticism and disappointment thrown at her. That's a lot for a child to deal with. For Leslie the pathway was to just give in and do what her mother had planned for her life. That didn't stop. As Leslie got older, it just got worse. Her mother's favorite statement was, "Leslie, you don't want to disappoint mother, do you?"

I met Leslie at a convention where I was speaking. My topic that day was centered around the thought *God has placed all of us on this earth to have three things – happiness, personal fulfillment and freedom.*

I had finished and the people who wanted to talk to me had all gone, except one – Leslie. She was seated on the edge of the stage just staring at me. I could feel the confusion she was wrestling with. I walked over, sat down beside her, looked her in the eyes and said, "You are one troubled young lady."

She looked at me and the tears just started flowing. "I have been that way all my life."

She paused, forced a smile through the tears and said in an emotional voice, "Well, I guess if I take what you said seriously, I don't have a life. I have an existence. The more I think about that, the truer I know it is. I am existing in a career I hate; I get up each morning to face a world I don't enjoy; I just want to crawl into bed, pull the covers over my head and stay there. Now, does that sound like I am living a life of happiness, fulfillment and freedom?"

"No. It sounds like you are existing in a world that someone else planned for you, and you have accepted it, rather than fighting for your unique place in life."

"Boy, did you hit that nail on the head. I don't have a life. I have an existence in a picture my mother painted for me. I really am in a career I hate. I know you are going to ask, *then, why are you in that career?* My mother picked it for me because it was safe and I could make good money. She was right; I am making great money, but what good is the money if you are not having fun? I just simply get up, go to work and do the things I need to do. I am intelligent enough and have enough smarts to make things happen. I have learned you can be good at something, make money, BUT not enjoy what you are doing."

"Your words are very true. The challenge is that word 'BUT.'" It is a big word. Why don't you confront your mother and tell her how you feel?"

"Believe me, I have. Each time I hear the same thing from her. *Honey, you don't want to disappoint mother, do you?* Those words create so much guilt for me. I want to stand up to her, but I can't. I just can't! I feel like my whole life is a detour that just keeps taking me further and further from what I really want to be doing."

"What is it you really want to be doing?"

"I want to pursue my acting career. That is what brings me the happiness, fulfillment and sense of freedom you were talking about. That is what I really want to be doing. I guess after my mother dies, I will do it then."

I wish others could have been there and felt the pain, seen the sadness and watched a life that was wasting away. Over the next year Leslie and I worked together to gain the freedom she needed to live her dream. It meant she had to face her mother and not allow the guilt to push her back to a life of detours. It meant she had to rewrite her personal script and give herself permission to live, rather than exist. That was challenging because she had never been in control of her life. Her life was her mother's plan she was living out. Today, Leslie is living her dream. Is she getting rich? No, but she is experiencing personal happiness, fulfillment and feels free to be herself.

Detours take life away; they don't give a person a sense of living with purpose. Detours steal the most valuable gift one has – time. Each day a person spends traveling the wrong road it narrows the possibility of them reaching their life's ultimate purpose. One can't expand their horizon traveling the wrong road. The wrong road will always take one in the wrong direction.

Expanding a person's horizon is also about framing their picture. One will either frame their journey with an emotional or mental border. The emotional border is about restrictions; the mental border is about expansion.

Most start with an emotional framing and work to get to the mental. This creates a very challenging journey. Starting from the point of emotional framing means one has to work through all the reasons *they can't* in order to get to why *they can.* It is not only the long way around; it is the most exhausting. Daily, one will find self wresting with negative feelings, rather than positive thoughts. Most people are not disciplined enough to get through the emotions they will have to face.

What they fail to understand is it is not just one set of emotions. If that were the case, they could do it. The wrestling match is with all the emotions they have collected, stored and keep reliving. That is the challenge. Each time they deal with one set of emotions, the rest come racing into the picture. They can't see the end result because of the clouds of confusion all these sets of emotions create. What happens? The thought of a possibility excites them, but the picture of the possibility gets buried under all the negatives that get thrown at them. Soon, the excitement turns to disappointment, which zaps their energy and leaves them without the strength to fight on. The result becomes them looking around, seeing what looks like another possibility and reaching for it. What looks like another possibility is just another detour that takes them further and further from the road to real success.

If one starts with mental framing, they find their imagination planning the journey. One's imagination is always about seeing the end result. One's imagination is about sketching the direct road map they will use. That doesn't mean there won't be hills, valleys, potholes and mountains to climb. They will be present, but rather than one seeing them as an obstacle, they will see them as an opportunity.

When one is guided by their imagination, they face their life with an "I will" attitude. When one is guided by their emotions, they will face their life with an "I'll try" attitude. The difference is more than the words; it is the sight plan they create. It can be seen in the behaviors one brings to the journey.

"I'll try" is not a positive statement. If a person really looks deep into what they are saying, they will find "trying" filled with doubt and uncertainty. The framing they are using is not filled with belief; it is grounded in a lack of self trust. That means each step they take has an emotional framing they will have to fight through. Again, most people aren't mentally strong enough to make it through this emotional mine field. They will start, but when disappointment, fatigue and a lack of energy take over, they will look for the first bail out point. That means just another detour designed to steal their time, their dream and their life. This is not about expanding their horizon; it is about giving up and simply accepting what is. That is not living.

Drew is a person who lives with a lot of desire, but not a strong imagination. His entire life had been based on trying and walking away. This had been his pattern for as long as he could remember. I met him at an Ace Hardware Convention where I was speaking.

I was standing outside the room and saw him coming with this big smile on his face. When he was about six steps from me he asked, "When are you leaving?"

"Tomorrow afternoon."

"How about I buy you breakfast in the morning. I promise I will talk your ears off."

I couldn't resist his honesty, so I said, "I eat early. I will meet you at 6:30 sharp in the restaurant."

"I'll be there. Rest tonight, because I have a lot to say to you."

When I arrived the next morning, he was already waiting. He wasn't joking about talking my ears off. Before we were even seated, his mouth was moving a mile a minute.

"Richard, I have been tripping over myself for years and I am tired of it. I know what I want, but just can't seem to get there. I feel like such a huge failure, but I know I am not. I look at what I haven't done and then at what I have done and I know I have a good life. I just don't have a fun life. Does that make sense to you?"

"Yes! I see people in that trap all the time. They have things that make them feel good for a moment; they just don't have the journey that will make them feel great about who they are, where they are and what they are doing with their life."

"That's it! I feel good about my life; I just don't feel great about it. I know there is more for me in this life, but I just can't find it."

"But, can you see it? Being able to see it is actually more important than being able to feel it. When all you can do is feel it, you are stifled. You know it is out there. You just don't know where. I'll bet you are one frustrated man."

"Frustrated," he chuckled. "I am beyond frustrated. I am 55 and know I don't have much time to make this thing happen."

"What thing?"

"That's where I am stuck. I feel it is there, I just can't see what it is. Am I crazy?"

"No, the good news is you are normal; the bad news is you are normal."

The look on his face said that didn't make a bit of sense to him. "Got you confused, don't I," I said as the grin spread across my face.

"Yep! You got me with that one."

"Drew, are you familiar with Stephen Covey?"

"Yes; I have read most of his books."

"I'll bet you have read <u>The 7 Habits Of Highly Effective People</u>?"

"Yes, I have read it several times."

"Do you remember the part about starting with the end in mind?"

"I think so."

"That is such a key component to getting your life in sync. It is such an important part of finding the difference between confusion and clarity. When you plan a trip, you need to know where you are going. If you don't, you will waste a lot of time, energy and fuel."

"Boy, have I done that. I am tired most of the time, feel like I am living on a track that is just one big circle and just feel totally lost."

"Drew, you have to change your framing. You have got

to get beyond feeling there is something out there for you to be able to see it."

"Okay; how do I do that? Where do I start?"

"It starts with your passion. What is it that really lights your inner fire? I mean if you could do anything you knew you had the talents to do, what would it be?"

"That's a good question. If I could do anything I knew I had the talent to do, what would it be? Want me to be honest with you?"

"I sure do."

"I love antiques. I would love to buy them, fix them up and sell them. I am really good with seeing the beauty in a piece of furniture.

"Drew, that is what I am talking about. When you look at an antique, you see what the end result could be."

"You're right! I do. I can look at a piece of furniture and see the beauty that could result in a little restoration. I have to tell you that really lights my fire. I get so excited."

"Why don't you do it?"

"Time; I don't have time."

"Is that a truth or a reason?"

"That's an interesting way of putting it. When you put it that way, I guess it is a reason. If I wanted this as much as I say I do, I would have the time for it. Oh, I get it! What I have been doing is feeling this is something I could do, not knowing this is something I want to do and seeing it as something I will do."

"You are so right. You have been lost in feeling this is something you could do, not committed to this being something you want to do. That is the difference. When you look at it, your framing is all emotions. Those emotions keep you staring at why it wouldn't work. Until you can get beyond your emotional framing and let your imagination come alive, all you are going to do is exist, and I mean exist, in a world where your emotions hold you a hostage to your dream."

Today Drew is purchasing, restoring and selling antiques. Every email I get from him is a *thank you* for helping him expand his horizon. Most limitations are not the result of desire, but a lack of mental sight. When the end result is planned in one's imagination, it will draw the picture of the journey. Yes, it will be tested. Yes, there will be moments of doubt; no, it is not an automatic thing. It will still demand persistent consistency based on consistent persistency. BUT, with the horizon expanded by being able to see where one is going, there is a great probability they will get there.

Don't forget – *when one's emotions are designing the framing, they will bring behaviors to their life that justify that design. When one's imagination is creating the framing, their imagination will implement behaviors that will clear the pathway and allow them to see the desired result clearly.*

## PRINCIPLES FOR EXPANDING YOUR HORIZON

1. Don't let others plan your journey; it is your life to plan.

2. Remember that all detours are a time thief.

3. If you are moving mentally and emotionally faster than you can manage, you are out of control.

4. While your emotions will speed you up, your imagination will slow you down.

5. Your emotions create possibilities, while your imagination shows you opportunities.

6. If all you are going to do is try, don't start the journey.

7. When you feel doubt, stop and find the source and face it.

8. Confront your critics and reach out to your support system.

9. Life is about you having happiness, personal fulfillment and a sense of freedom.

10. Study your behavior; it will show you your real agenda.

Chapter 8

# No One To Blame, Except Me

**Step Three: Holding Yourself Accountable**

*Until you can face your life with a sense of honesty, you will find yourself having to justify all those things you know you shouldn't have done or continue to do.*

The third step in the process of balancing ones words with their behavior requires *holding yourself accountable*. This is just as important as the first two. There is no one aspect of this process that is any less important than the other parts. Personal accountability is a GIANT piece to this puzzle.

Earlier we talked about the missing of accountability in our society today. Where there is no accountability there is no reason for a person to face their behavior.

Of all the stories I have learned while spending time in people's lives none is more to the point than the situation I was part of in St. Louis a few years ago.

I was at the Adams Mark Hotel downtown to speak to a network marketing convention. My program time was scheduled for 7:30 in the evening for 90 minutes. Those who know me know it is rare for me to speak in the evening. The challenge I have is most programs run late and the people are normally tired.

They wanted me backstage at 7:00 so I would be in place for my 7:30 presentation. I was told it was important for me to be there because they were committed to running on time. Those words always sound great to me, but many times when a person is given the microphone who has always wanted their six minutes of fame, they forget about the six minutes.

On this Saturday evening I had agreed to do the keynote address. Well, as things would be, the program ran late. Well, 7:30 came and went; 8:30 came and disappeared; 9:30 and 10:30 soon passed by. It was 11:21 p.m. when they started introducing me. Back stage I am telling myself, "Richard, there is no way you can take 90 minutes this late in the evening. They have been in their seats since 6:45 p.m. They have to be exhausted."

I walked out on stage and spent 18 minutes talking about what I feel is the most important issue in life — *personal honesty.* I have always thought until a person gets honest with self, there is no way to improve their life.

The next morning I'm sitting in the restaurant working on a project when I catch this gentleman standing across the room staring at me. From years of working with behavior I knew what was about to happen. He needed to talk and I was the one he needed to talk to. I figured by the time I got my computer shut down he would be at my table.

As I closed my computer's lid, he was at my table. Before I could say anything to him, he blurted out, "Can I talk to you?"

"Certainly; sit down."

"No," was his reply as he took a sudden step back. "I didn't say I wanted to sit with you. I just need to talk to you. I was hoping I could find you here this morning. You're the reason I couldn't sleep last night. I have been sitting in my room arguing with you."

He paused, stepped toward me until he was literally in my face. In a very loud and angry tone he finished what he needed to say. "I've been lying to myself for forty years and you or no one else is going to change that fact."

With that he turned and walked out of my life. For a moment I watched him walk away and then reached for a sheet of paper and wrote this thought:

*If what you say you want is*
*contradicted by what you do,*
*you are lying to yourself and*
*all the people you have said it to.*

To balance words and behavior one must hold self accountable for what they say and what they do. Until they are willing to take this step, they will always find a way to justify their behavior. The challenge is they get by with it. Without accountability there is no reason for a person to do anything differently. When one's behavior is not confronted, it is validated. The validation is the permission they use to continue their self-destructive journey.

For anyone to improve there must be accountability for their behavior. They must know what behaviors are acceptable and which are not. Without accountability any statement of consequence is simply a lie. Why is it so challenging to hold people accountable?

One reason is the fear of confrontation. Most people have a fear of confrontation. They see it as negative, when in reality, confrontation is the skill of resolution. It is not about winning or losing; it is about resolving the event. Confrontation is putting the issue in front of all those involved and working together to create a common agenda.

Most of the conflict I have seen is the result of people having a personal agenda they won't let go of. It doesn't matter about being right or wrong, they just want to hang onto what they are feeling.

When there is no common agenda, there is no pathway to resolve the issue. Without resolution there is continuation and the continuation will lead to even greater conflict that will strengthen into criticism.

Ruth was a sweetheart, but at the same time was a doormat for most of the people in her life. Most everyone in her life, including her husband and children, just flat ran over her. They treated her with disrespect and joked about how weak she was behind her back.

She was an emotional mess when she came to me. Recently, her husband had embarrassed her with a put down joke in front of a group of their friends. That was more than she could take. Her words to me were filled with anger and hurt and her tone was over the edge.

"I just can't believe he would do that in front of all those people," she shouted in a tone of anger. There was a long pause and then in a lower tone, "I guess I am not being honest. I shouldn't be surprised. He has treated me that way for years. He treats me with so much disrespect."

"Why do you let him do that to you?"

"Because that is who he is."

"That may be who he is, but it is also who you let him be to you. When he treats you with disrespect, why don't you confront him? Why don't you hold him accountable for his behavior?"

"Are you kidding? He would kill me."

"Well, it sounds like that is what he is doing to you right now. As long as you let him treat you that way, he will. You have to stand up to him if there is to be any improvement. I mean the question is real simple – *are you going to continue to allow him to beat you down and you become less and less of a person?"*

"The answer is I don't want to be treated that way, but it is not as simple as that."

"Why?"

" Because, that is how he has always been."

"No and Yes! Yes, that is who he has become, but no, it doesn't have to continue to be that way. All behavior is consistent with how you tell people they can treat you. He treats you like you ask to be treated and will continue until you confront him. Don't you deserve to be treated better than that?"

125

"Yes, I do, but I am fearful of saying anything to him. I tried once and he just used my feelings against me. He told me to grow up and stop whining like a baby. I told myself I would never do that again."

"Then, Ruth, you are trapped. If you can't confront his behavior, you have to accept it. If you accept it, then you live in his prison and have to suffer the consequences that go with that acceptance. I know it wouldn't be easy to confront him, but it is the only way out. I would be willing to help you, but you have to really want this. When I sit down with the two of you, he will be angry. People like him don't like to be held accountable for their behavior. Their ability to intimidate keeps most people from confronting their behavior. The strength of their ability to intimidate heightens the fear of confrontation. They are because they are given permission to be that way."

"I don't know if I can do what you are suggesting."

"You know the result of not confronting him. Think about it and let me know what you want to do."

Ruth never confronted her husband. It was always sad to see her. Her body language was one of a beaten woman.

Confrontation is all about resolving issues by holding people accountable for their actions, their behaviors.

Others fear confrontation because of being rejected. Over and over I have had people say to me, "If I confront them, they won't like me." They didn't understand the message disrespect sends is one that says, "I don't like you." People you like and/or respect get treated with respect. Remember, *Behavior Never Lies!*

Others resist confronting because they know their behavior will be called into question. The greatest escape from being held accountable is blame. As long as it is someone else's fault, they don't have to take responsibility for what is. As long as they can blame another person, they don't have to be accountable. The challenge is *this has become an acceptable way of life.* Too many are protected, rather than made accountable for their behavior.

So many times when I was serving as the Minister of Counseling on the church staff, I would get calls from the county jail about a young person that had been arrested. I would talk to them and then talk to the parents. It's unbelievable the number of times parents would protect their child from facing the consequences of their behavior.

I will never forget Stuart. He was a spoiled brat; he had been arrested for street racing. His parents had bought him a new car and he was showing off. Sitting in the cell, he looked at me with a smug look on his face and said, "This is no big deal. My mom and dad will be here shortly and take care of all this."

When his parents showed up, their presence was just like his – defiant and argumentative with the police. Watching his dad, I knew there would be no consequences to his son's behavior. I followed what happened and sure enough there were no consequences.

Stuart's words, "This is no big deal" are too frequent. Stuart's father commented, "Kids will be kids. There is nothing wrong with that" are too often spoken and accepted. Without accountability, one can blame their way out of anything. Hey, there is always a reason, an excuse, a justification or someone or something to blame for behavior. Reality is, most statements of avoidance are not designed to hold one accountable nor force them to face the truth. They are designed to make blame okay. For words and behavior to be in sync there must be accountability.

## PRINCIPLES FOR ACCOUNTABILITY

1.  Blame cannot be accepted as justification for behavior.

2.  There must be consequences to behavior that are implemented.

3.  Without accountability there is chaos.

4.  Behavior must be confronted.

5.  Resolution must have a stronger presence than fear.

6.  Accountability must be consistent; no exceptions.

7.  Focusing on growth demands accountability.

8.  Discipline and accountability are first cousins.

9.  Any behavior you haven't confronted has been validated.

10. Remember, each day you either choose to feed your confusion or strengthen your clarity; your behavior is the real definition of your choice.

Chapter 9

# Consistently Inconsistent

---

### Step Four: Addressing Your Inconsistencies

---

*Inconsistencies create the contradictions that keep you at war with yourself.*

The next step in this process demands *addressing your inconsistencies with action.* An excuse is always made by a person giving self permission to make the excuse. Excuses are not accidental statements. As long as excuses are seen as okay, one will not challenge their behavior. They must move beyond their world of good intentions. I have found that for most people good intentions are just another form of an excuse. With good intentions tomorrow becomes the place where the person is going to start doing what they have known they should be doing. Oh, I think there is desire in the statement; it just hasn't been agreed to emotionally.

When one really listens to why a person didn't "Get to it," they can hear the excuse and blame that is being used. As long as one gives self permission to procrastinate, they will. The challenge is many have convinced themselves that they really are going to do it. They have become so ingrained in their lie; they actually see it as truth. They haven't fully understood those three little words – *Behavior Never Lies.*

The only way to get beyond this and create the balance between what is said and what is done is to face the inconsistency that good intentions create and take positive action.

Most people called Ralph, "Mr. Good Intentions." He didn't like it, but he knew it was true about him. He would joke about it, but inside he was at war with self. He came to me as what he called, "My last resort."

I had known him for several years and had watched his erratic behavior. He had a great heart and really meant to do most of the things he promised to do. He just never seemed to get around to anything.

On several occasions I heard him tell people, "You can

count on me. I know I haven't been very good in the past, but I have turned over a new leaf. I will get it done."

They would smile, nod their head and walk away. Well, nine times out of ten he didn't get it done. The result was a growing disbelief from people toward him. Over a period of time people stopped counting on him. They just didn't believe what he would tell them.

When he asked if we could talk, I jumped at the opportunity. It was one of those rare times when I was doing a program in my own hometown. I don't do that too often, because when I go home I want to get away from people.

"Ralph, why do you make promises and then not keep them? Don't you know yourself well enough to know to not do that?"

"Richard, I really mean to do it. I know you may not believe me, but I do mean it; when I say it, I really do."

"But Ralph, Behavior Never Lies. If you meant to do it, you would have gotten it done."

"I know your three little words and yes, you are right."

"Ralph, I know you don't mean to lie, but when you make a promise and then don't keep it, people soon stop believing in you. Why do you do that to yourself? Are you too scattered? Is it hard for you to stay focused?"

"I am very scattered. I start a lot of things and either run into a wall and not know what to do or I get bored with what I am doing. When I get bored, I just walk away."

"Do you work on more than one thing at a time?"

"Yes; I have at least four projects going at the same time."

"Could that be part of your challenge? Maybe when you look at what you have to do, you don't see just what is in front of you; you see everything there is for you to do and feel overwhelmed."

"I think I do that a lot. Most days I look around and don't know where to start. When that happens, I will touch a couple of things and then throw up my hands in disgust and walk away."

"Ralph, that is the behavior you have to correct. You have to take things one at a time. You complete it and then take on another project. You are a personality that doesn't perform well when you see stacks that need your attention. You would rather just leave the clutter and go start something new. All that does is add to your stacks of incomplete tasks. You must learn that anything that doesn't have completion has continuation. Ralph, just because you don't complete what you start, doesn't mean you have turned loose of it. Your mind doesn't release anything until it is completed. Does that make sense to you?"

"Sure does. I have mastered the art of starting and stopping, starting and stopping. Now, I need to master the behavior of completing. I must learn to resist me telling myself I am going to do this and look at what I am really doing. This is going to take some work."

"It is going to take you slowing down and listening to what you are saying. You have to stop jumping because you think someone or something needs you. You have to take positive action and complete what you start before you move to the next project."

People look at me funny when I say this, but I really believe it. *A person knows what they need to do.* It is a rare occasion that I have someone bring their challenge to me that doesn't know what they really need to do. They want me to give them permission to do what they already know they should be doing, SO if things don't workout, they have an escape path. When one can use, "I was only doing what he told me to do," as their justification, they feel they are not responsible for the outcome. Many have been angry with me when I would not play their game. They would present their challenge and I would follow with a series of questions that put the responsibility back on them.

I remember one occasion when a lady I was counseling got so angry at me she leaped out of her chair onto the top of my desk. She was on her hands and knees screaming at me, "I don't like you; I don't like you! You call yourself a counselor. You aren't helping me; you don't care about me. If you did, you would tell me what to do."

My response was, "Because I care about you and want to help you with the situation you are challenged by is the reason I won't tell you what to do. You want me to be responsible for your life, and I won't do that. This is not my challenge; it is yours. My role is to guide you in the right direction. I am not here to be your answer. You know what you need to do; you just don't want to face your life with honesty. Until you can do that, you will remain trapped in your life the way it is. Now, if you don't mind, get down off my desk and let's continue our discussion. If you can't handle my counseling style, I am sure you can find someone who will play your game, BUT that person is not going to be me."

She got down off my desk and we continued our working together for the next few months. I will never forget the day she stopped me in the church hallway and said, "I am so sorry I treated you the way I did. You were right. I wanted you to be responsible for my life. Thank you for not doing that. You made me face my life and make an honest decision within myself. I had to choose whether I was going to continue to run by making others the reason or face my life and see myself as the real challenge. I chose to face myself and stop this life of inconsistencies and move forward. Thank you for being honest and being real with me."

One knows what action they need to take to get through the jungle of confusion they have created for themselves and have chosen not to face. The answer they are seeking is really within them; they just have to be willing to listen to their inner voice as it whispers to them and then implement the positive action. That voice lives inside each of us. It speaks to us when it knows our behavior is taking us in the wrong direction. Call it consciousness, intuition or whatever name is given to it, but that inner voice is there to speak to us when we are moving at a speed or in a direction that is taking us away from what we have said is our plan. The challenge is getting a person to slow down and really pay attention to what it is telling us. Too many times we hear that inner voice and just dismiss what it is saying. Then, and it is a big THEN, we find ourselves struggling with the decision we made.

How many times have we told ourselves something like, "I knew better," "I can't believe I did that. How stupid could I have been?" "What was I thinking? I knew this was wrong when I did it."

A person really is designed to achieve what they are achieving. I have said that for years and each time I see the look on people's faces saying, "I don't understand what you are saying." Truth is truth and there is no denying the lesson truth holds. There is no one to blame for what one does with their life. Yes, others may exert influence or push their opinions on another person, but in the end it is the individuals choice to accept or reject what they have heard.

Blame has become much too acceptable in our society. Having a reason why one's life is messed up and not wanting to be held accountable for their behavior has become a way of life. The truth is, *YOU and only YOU is responsible for your life*. The confusion, the inconsistencies, the behaviors are all the result of what one chooses to do. With each choice there is a journey; when one makes the decision, they accept the journey that goes with it. That means it is theirs! The devil didn't make them do it; hey, he may have created the temptation, but the person made the choice. As much as they would like to use another person as their escape route, the responsibility for "what is" falls squarely back on their shoulders.

An inconsistency is a contradiction between what a person says and what they do. When the two are not in sync, there is going to be conflict. A person's behavior will affect others. For one to think they are the lone ranger is a BIG misconception. Anyone who stands in a person's life will either be part of or feel the repercussions of the choice they have made.

Inconsistencies keep a person scattered. They start something, don't complete it and move on to something else. The situation they started, but didn't complete doesn't just lie there without any emotional connection. The person's mind knows it isn't completed yet and keeps bringing it back to their attention. The mind is so interesting; it keeps a checklist of things started and not completed and will not let one forget it is still there.

Inconsistencies create stacks of clutter. Clutter becomes the mental, emotional and physical piles of the incomplete stacks. Clutter creates emotional reactions; one knows the clutter is there and each time they have to face the clutter they wrestle with all the emotions associated with whatever the stack contains.

Inconsistencies become the largest point of distractions. It doesn't matter whether it is mental, emotional or physical, the stacks will become distractions. One can be looking or working on anything and still sense or feel the incomplete stacks. These distractions destroy focus, drains energy and wears a person down. The result is one loses their consistent persistency, because they are no longer persistently consistent.

## PRINCIPLES OF CONTROLLING INCONSISTENCIES

1. Never start a project until you know you are ready to see it through.

2. Learn the power of saying "no" and don't be afraid to say it.

3. Don't let others dump on you what they don't want to do.

4. Don't let your ego make you feel you are a super human and can do it all.

5. Refuse to just touch things; complete what you start.

6. Don't do things because you are excited; do them because you are enthusiastic.

7. Understand the time requirements for the things you are going to do.

8. Create a plan that is realistic.

9. If you really aren't going to do it, don't let it just lie there; put it or throw it away.

10. Don't jump in with both feet; walk in focused on the task and committed to doing it.

*BEHAVIOR NEVER LIES*

Chapter 10

# Trust Your Fan Club

## Step Five: Very Carefully Align Yourself With The Right People

*The wrong people offer you a wrong direction; the right people take you in the right direction.*

The next piece to this puzzle is about how one must *very carefully align self with people who challenge, not criticize them.* Have you ever had someone in your life who liked, rejoiced, in being able to show you what you had or were doing wrong? They pretended to be your friend, but used that pretense to attack you on every occasion they had.

These people are so interesting. They begin with, "I hope you don't take what I am about to say wrong, but..." or "I am only saying this to help you" or they will frame it this way, "I am only telling you this because I am your friend."

The reality is none of these pretense statements are true. They have an agenda and it does not contain an attitude of love. Their agenda is self-motivated and is usually guided by envy, anger or jealousy. Remember something we talked about earlier? *All behavior has an agenda.* That is such an important thought for one to remember. These people will disguise their motive in a cloak of concern. Reality is, the cloak is a lie. They don't care about the person they are criticizing; in fact a negative agenda has only one purpose – *to inflict hurt.* When one realizes that, the strength of the three words, *Behavior Never Lies*, takes on a new meaning in their life.

It is a sad thought, but true; most people who enter a person's life are not there to help them. They are there to either use their good heart or to break it. I hope there is a clear understanding to what I am saying. Envy, anger and jealousy are such powerful negative emotions. The behaviors these emotions evoke are both ugly and dangerous.

I have taught for years the thought *the more a person wants to achieve the more of a loner they have to become.* That is one of the BIG price tags to personal improvement. It is also one of the stumbling blocks that keep many from reaching the plan they have stated they want for their life. When one is surrounded with people who don't support their dream, those people's negative energy can make it very challenging to achieve their dream. The more committed one is to improving their life, the more enemies they are going to create.

Improving requires each person becoming particular with who they let remain in their life. If a person isn't particular, they will find their life filled with people whose mission is to make sure they don't achieve their agenda of personal growth/personal achievement.

Why is it so challenging for most people to accept the fact that negative people have an agenda? That agenda is not about helping a person improve; it is about finding their faults and constantly throwing them at the person. Their agenda is about working to destroy one's focus with negative questions that create doubt. They have mastered the art of using guilt to make one question whether their commitment to growth is really fair. Negative people can rip one's dream apart with their destructive presence. They don't want the individual to grow; they don't want them to improve. They can make the good look bad and growth seem like a negative part of life. Don't ever underestimate their power; they are intelligent, cunning and able to control the pictures a person looks at to create the journey for their life.

What do I mean by the statement, "You have to be particular with who you let remain in your life?" Simply stated, it means *don't keep anyone in your life who is not part of your fan club.*

See how this ties into the thought *the more you want to achieve with your life the more of a loner you have to become?* This is not about a person being better than others.

141

It is about one protecting self from those whose agenda is to use them for their own personal gain. It is about one creating an environment where their growth and personal discovery is made possible by surrounding their life with people who share a common agenda of personal discovery and achievement. It is about sharing their environment with people whose behavior is consistent with their stated agenda. One doesn't have to worry about these people stealing their energy. One doesn't have to worry about emotionally fighting with these people; they share a common journey and a common agenda of growth. These become one's support center filled with trust and truth that allows anything to be discussed and resolved.

Hear me and accept what I am saying as truth. People either add to a life with their presence, or steal from that life through manipulating with their hidden agenda. One has to become savvy enough to sense the agenda and strong enough to not allow those who are there to steal from them to have a continuing presence in their life. They have to become a student of hearing people's behavior. The more one understands and accept those three words, *Behavior Never Lies*, the easier it will be for them to hear with their eyes the behavior of people. The more they believe that *Behavior Never Lies* the easier it will become for them to eliminate those who are only there to steal from their life.

I was in Sydney, Australia when I met Mandy. She was a lady with a million questions. I had spotted her in the audience because of the inquisitive look on her face throughout my presentation. I was sitting in the Café when she found me.

"I have been looking for you," she said with a big smile on her face.

"Well, I must not have done a very good job of hiding,"

I replied through a chuckle.

"I knew you had to be here somewhere. Do you mind if
I bug you for a few minutes?"

"No, be my guest. Sit down and be a bug for a little bit."

"Your presentation was very interesting," she said with
this serious look on her face. After a brief pause she continued,
"No, interesting is not the right word. It was very thought
provoking for me. It has been a long time since I have had
someone get that deep inside my mind. I found what you were
saying very prevalent for where I am right now. I am one of
those you talked about that is standing at a crossroad. I want
to improve my life. That is a quest I have been on for several
years now. I know deep inside me I can achieve this crusade
I am on. After your presentation today, I now understand the
#1 challenge I am facing is about some of the people who are
standing in my life right now. When you said, *Behavior Never
Lies*, you woke me up."

There was a pause filled with looks that told me she
was walking through the people who were closest to her life.
"I have mostly been a person who just trusted people. I never
wanted to believe that people could enter your life to hurt you.
I listened as you described the behavior of those who were
not part of your fan club and realized I have those people. I
can see how I have been part of their agenda and they haven't
been part of mine. Thank you for opening my eyes to the fact
of *Behavior Never Lies*. I have to go back and do some people
house cleaning."

There was another pause followed by a smile that
looked more like a smirk. "Maybe I need to take your advice
and take them to lunch and order theirs to go."

We both chuckled, but I could see the relief in her eyes.

143

She was now clear on the connection between presence and behavior.

As she turned to leave, she looked back and said, "Thank you for helping me to understand the meaning of particular. If I am not particular, I will miss the people who are placed in my life as a gift. I know I have done that in the past and I won't be doing that anymore. Thank you and I really mean that."

There are lots of people who will enter a life, but that doesn't mean they should be allowed to take up residency. One should listen with their ears and their eyes in order to find those whose presence is about strengthening their presence.

Living in sync where words and behavior are together in meaning demand a person surround and fill their life with people who are with them on their journey, not in their life to make their journey difficult. These are the people who will challenge them with their presence of persistent consistency that is balanced with consistent persistency. These are the people who will stretch their imagination and challenge them to examine their beliefs. These are the people who will hold them accountable through caring, not criticizing. These are the people who will stand beside them with a caring presence when life turns upside down; one's fan club will greet them with a genuine caring and at the same time always be open and honest with their comments. They don't play games; they will celebrate the growth and confront the negative behavior. They are not part of one's life with a hidden agenda. Their time in the person's life may only be for a season, but they will have a presence that is present when they are no longer present.

## PRINCIPLES FOR ALIGNING YOURSELF WITH THE RIGHT PEOPLE

1.  Starts with you being strong in your beliefs.

2.  Never keep anyone in your life that doesn't appreciate your presence.

3.  Don't give time to critics.

4.  Revisit your dream on a daily basis.

5.  Be clear on what you want for your life.

6.  Don't be fearful of eliminating people who are part of your fan club.

7.  Be honest with yourself first and then with others.

8.  Listen with your eyes and your ears to those you respect.

9.  Remember, implementing what you learn keeps the right people coming to your life.

10. You have the right to choose who you want in your life; it is your life!

Chapter 11

# Time For A Wake-Up Call

## Step Six:  Increase Your Awareness

*The sharper your mental sight the easier it becomes to control your emotional reactions.*

Living in sync also means *increasing one's awareness*.
I was visiting with Lisa about the challenges with her life.
She is a very talented, intelligent and driven lady, BUT like so
many she keeps tripping over herself.

"There are times I don't understand myself," were her
words filled with disgust.

"Welcome to the world of human behavior. You are not
alone. I talk to people everyday that are totally disgusted with
self."

"Richard, I am not dumb. I am a very intelligent person
who can't seem to get beyond her self sabotage. I keep doing
the same things over and over that I told myself I wasn't going
to continue doing. I know better; I tell myself to slow down
and watch what I do. I know the drill. I understand what my
behavior is doing, BUT I just can't seem to stop myself. It is
like I get started, wake up to what I am doing, tell myself to
stop and just speed up."

"Yes, you know the drill; you know what you are doing,
but that doesn't mean you can simply control yourself doing
it."

"That doesn't make sense to me. I am intelligent
enough to figure things out."

"No question about that, but sometimes intelligence
and emotions don't operate with the same agenda. Your mind
knows what you need to do, but your emotions are ruling your
life. It is not a sign you lack intelligence. It is just the fact your
emotions are stronger than your mental strength. That is one of
the greatest challenges all of us face everyday. We know what
is right for us, but we don't listen to our self-talk. It seems that
when most of us are having a heart to heart talk with self, we
turn a deaf ear. Have you done that?"

"Yes, and it makes me so angry. I find myself doing the things I have said I am not going to do again. It is like I don't listen to me. I don't take what I know I need to do seriously. Just the thought of that makes me angry sitting here."

"You are right when you say you don't listen to yourself. You can't listen with your emotions. You listen with your mind. If your emotional presence is stronger than your mental sight, you are going to keep repeating the things you have said you weren't going to do anymore. Does that make sense to you?"

" Yes! It makes a lot of sense. It is like I am not aware of what I am doing until I am already doing it."

What Lisa was talking about is the challenge most people face. They live in such an emotionally driven world that their behavior becomes an automatic reaction. They are so driven by defining their life through their emotions; they just react and then, get frustrated with what they have done. Rather than facing that fact by slowing down, they speed up and give self a personal beating.

The challenge is for a person to expand their awareness. The key is to understand their emotional design, learn their triggers and not just jump in with both emotional feet.

Here is the challenge to learn. *Awareness is not a function of your emotions; it is a function of your mind.* A person's emotions just react, while their mind responds. Awareness demands a mental pace that allows one to see the total picture. When one is racing emotionally, they don't have the sight they need to see everything that is going on around them. They are staring at what is in front of them, not focusing on what is happening around their life. Awareness is one slowing down in order to have the peripheral vision necessary to see and respond to the total event.

SO, if one is an emotionally driven person, their ability to respond will be overshadowed by their reactions. They will jump in with both emotional feet and then, realize what they have done. At that point the thought of stopping, turning around and establishing a new direction is present, but is too emotionally overwhelming for them to deal with. So, what do they do? They either continue down the path they know is wrong with justifications or just give up and walk away with another stack of incomplete living in their life. Very few have the discipline to stop, turn and regroup.

Awareness demands a person think first. That requires the strength of discipline, the stamina of commitment and fine tuning of one's imagination.

I have said for years one of the great weakness of most people is they don't think. Most people don't think; they think they think. Reality is, they react, create a mess and either hand it off to someone to resolve or just walk away and create another pile of clutter in their life.

Awareness can't be an afterthought. If it occurs after one has emotionally jumped in with both feet, the likelihood of them being able to stop the destruction is very unlikely.

The key is to slow down and examine the behavior before it gets implemented. The question is, "Will this behavior strengthen or weaken the confusion my life?" If the behavior is about weakening their life, the response must be to not implement it. That takes awareness; that takes discipline; that takes a mental desire that is stronger than their emotional presence. A person must think about their behavior before it takes them to an emotional speed they can't control.

Awareness takes clear imagination. One of the great things about a person's imagination is it sees in pictures. There is nothing a life can be handed that their imagination can't see the pathway through. Now, I know many wouldn't agree with that statement. The reason they can't agree is they don't use their imagination as a source of clarity. Their imagination becomes a second choice. This goes back to the understanding that most react with their emotions, create a mess and then want their imagination to clean up the mess. This goes back to pace. They don't walk in looking for the solution; they race in just trying to get through the emotional jungle. They don't enter with an awareness of what is happening; they race in feeling what they think is wrong. When one enters with the wrong presence, they are going to go in the wrong direction.

Anytime one is confused about "what is," they must not speed up; they must slow the pace and examine everything, not just what they are feeling. Awareness demands a clear presence. That takes us back to pace. The faster one is moving emotionally, the less clarity they have. The less their clarity the more their confusion. Confusion will steal their awareness.

Russell is a great illustration of confusion created by a pace one can't manage with the result being a loss of understanding with what they are doing. I met him at a Robyn Thompson Real Estate Investors Bootcamp. I was outside the room waiting for my time to speak when Russell walked up to me. "You're Richard Flint."

"Yes, I am."

"Robyn talks about you all the time. She says you are the reason she is as successful as she is. Is that true?"

"Well, the answer to that question is both yes and no."

The look on his face said he didn't get it. I smiled and explained, "Robyn is the reason she is successful. My role in her life was to make her aware of where she was, what she was missing in her journey and help her discover the pathway beyond the confusion that was holding her hostage. She is the one who took the insights and implemented them into her life. I couldn't do that for her."

"Can you do that for anyone?"

"NO!"

Again, there was this puzzled look on his face as he stood there and just stared at me. I let him ponder for a second and continued. "I can't do it for anyone. They have to do it for themselves. My role is to guide those who are ready to stop talking about what they want to do and do it. If their mindset is right and their desire is stronger than their fear, I can take them there."

"Could you tell by talking to me if I am ready?"

"Yes! I can ask you a few questions and know whether your words are simply words or a statement of your desire."

"Could we talk after your presentation?"

"I'll meet you here one hour after I finish."

Later when we sat down, the look on his face was one of fear and excitement. He was like a little kid who was excited, but afraid to ask the question. "I listened to you today and you were talking right to me. I am the person who is so scattered I am an emotional wreck. I want to succeed in this business and I know I can. I just can't seem to figure out what aspect of real estate investing I want to do. I listen to one person talk and think that that is my niche'. Then, the next speaker talks about another aspect and I think that is what I want to do. Each time I come to one of these meetings I get even more confused."

"Do you understand that is most of the people in that room? They are confused, scattered and spend most days working against what they say they want. They are trapped in their confusion. Everything they hear is what they now feel they want to do. They aren't aware of the need to slow down, find their calling and reach for it."

"Why is that such a challenge? I know what you are saying, but I can't seem to accept it. Does that make sense?"

"Absolutely! You are hungry to achieve success, but haven't figured out which highway to take to get there. So, what do you do? You figure you will try each highway for a short time and find the one that is the most appealing. The challenge with that is the time you are wasting. Each highway you travel that ends up being a detour has just cost you time, money, energy and left you with more uncertainty. You have to slow down and examine, not experiment with everything. Experimenting doesn't increase your awareness and understanding; it actually dulls it. Does that statement make sense to you?"

"I think so."

"Too many make what they think is a decision, when in reality they have created a moment of touch and not created a journey to improve their life. The key is to slow down and *really* examine each aspect of the industry that you have an interest in, talk to people who are involved in that aspect and then, decide if this is the right part of the industry for you. Without the research you are only creating more confusion for your life. With the research you become more aware and are able to focus your energy on a journey, not a distraction."

Russell is like so many people in life. They are curious, not sure. There is a huge difference. Yes, journeys begin because a person is curious, but if the curiosity is not taken to clarity before they start, they will end up on a detour, rather than a journey. For one's emotions and their mind to be in sync there has to be clarity. It is the clarity that allows one's mind to have a stronger presence than their emotions.

## PRINCIPLES FOR INCREASING YOUR AWARENESS

1. Walk; don't run.

2. Seek clarity by asking the right questions to the right people.

3. Sort out your emotions; don't let them sink into confusion.

4. Make sure you have the information you need before you start.

5. Don't be strictly driven by your emotions.

6. Pause when you feel you are moving too fast.

7. Awareness demands clarity, so do your research.

8. Refuse to run with others who are moving too fast.

9. Don't be afraid to let your imagination play with an idea.

10. Stop when you feel confused, overwhelmed or very uncertain.

Chapter 12

# Not So Fast

## Step Seven:  Operating Your Life At A Manageable Pace

*Either you are managing your life
or your life is managing you.*

Living with one's mind and emotions being in sync requires *operating at a manageable pace*. This fits hand in hand with what we have been talking about. Reality is, either one's mind or emotions are ruling their life. Whichever has the strongest presence is making the rules they are living by. If they want to know which is in control, all they have to do is examine the pace of their life.

A person's mind will slow them down, expand their awareness and move them toward resolving the situation. The slower they are moving mentally, the more awareness they have; the greater their awareness the calmer they are; the calmer they are the more clarity they have about what must be done. The result is them implementing behaviors designed to allow them to manage their life, rather than their life managing them.

When one is living with their emotions guiding their life, the opposite is true. It is amazing how life can turn into a race when one is being guided by their emotions. They look at what they think is happening; at that point what they think is happening is not reality. They are not thinking; they are just dealing with their feelings. As much as they may feel they are making a decision, they are not! Feelings, by their self, can't make a decision; they can only create a moment.

Decisions are the process of the mind seeing the pathway toward solution and moving in that direction. Feelings see through a vale of emotions, which means one doesn't have clarity. They only have what they feel is happening. When one is only using their emotions, they are clouded and lacking the clarity needed to make a decision that creates freedom and allows them to move forward without having to walk backwards into yesterday and face the situation again.

How many times do people think they were finished

with something only to have it reappear? Each time it reappears the emotions connected to it are stronger and more challenging to work through. The more times one has to face the same issue the more frustrated they become. The greater their frustrations the faster they move emotionally. The result is their emotions managing their life, rather than their imagination. When that happens, the pace will send them out of control.

To live a life where words and behavior are working with each other, not against each other, one has to be moving at a pace they can manage. When the pace is unmanageable, so is life!

Cindy is a great example of the battle between one's mind and their emotions being in conflict and what it does to the pace of their life. Her opening words to me were not new, but filled with a jungle of emotional entanglements.

"Richard, I can't live like this anymore. All of this is killing me."

I knew her and knew what she was talking about. Her husband was one of the most cunning people a person could ever meet. He was a master at using pity or fear to get what he wanted. He knew how to create a sad story so everyone felt sorry for him. He was so masterful at telling it, everyone believed what he was saying.

He was also a master at using fear to control. He had a temper he knew how to turn off and on in order to make others back away. They didn't want to incur his wrath.

For sixteen years he had terrorized her and the kids. Since he was a boy, he had created stories that made him the victim and everyone else the villain. When Cindy left him, she thought she would be free of the pain and torture he brought to their life. The reality was it increased.

He went to all their "so-called" friends and told them

how she had left him; he was so convincing these "so-called" friends were calling Cindy wanting to know "how could you do that to him?" These people had no idea of the hell she had been through. Cindy was not one to wash her laundry in public.

When he had time with the kids, he would terrorize them and threaten them if they didn't tell him everything that was going on in Cindy's life. They would go home and tell her. She would get angry at what he was doing, BUT was so fearful of him she wouldn't confront his behavior. All that did was reinforce the fact he could control her through fear. So, what did he do? He increased the intensity of his presence through fear. The result was Cindy falling apart emotionally, mentally and physically. Each time she would go to see her doctor the message was the same, "Cindy you can't live under this pressure. If you don't resolve what is going on in your life, you are going to kill yourself."

Cindy knew the truth of his words. She could feel herself dying from the inside out. Now, one might think, "What is wrong with this person? Why doesn't she deal with this?"

Until one has been terrorized by fear and feel there is nothing they can do, they don't understand the trauma the Cindy's live with. It wasn't that Cindy didn't want to deal with what was happening, she was so emotionally paralyzed she couldn't see things being any different. She was emotionally moving so fast there was no time for her mind to have a moment of control. When she did try to slow down and start to face her life with positive resolve, he would sense it and increase his emotional attacks. The result was her getting knocked backward and all the progress she had made getting sucked out of her.

Each time she and I would talk I would ask her, "Cindy, when are you going to stand up to him? You know each time you let him knock you down, your emotional entanglements increase and the pace of your life becomes more unmanageable. You know that!"

"I know; I know," would be her hurried response. "I am going to deal with it, but I waiting for the right time."

Her response was based in her fear. The fear was so strong it didn't allow her to hear what she was really saying through her behavior.

"Cindy, when do you think the right time will be? Will it be today, tomorrow and next year? When do you think it will be?"

"I don't know," was her emotional response. "I just can't deal with this right now. I am not strong enough. Anyway, if I stand up to him, he is going to take it out on the kids. I won't do that to them. I would rather live in this continuing hell than put them through that."

What she didn't completely understand was the strength she needed would be there when she slowed her emotions down and allowed her mind to show her the pathway she needed to travel. As long as she was being completely guided by her emotions, they were creating an unmanageable pace for her life. At the emotional speed she was moving, she would be dead before this was resolved.

There are a lot of Cindy's out there who live with an emotional pace that is dangerous to their mental, emotional and physical health. They know what they need to do, but the depth of their emotional entanglements is so strong they become paralyzed through a pace they can't manage. The result is their inner spirit being sucked out of them. The weaker their inner spirit, the more challenging it becomes to slow their life down and implement the behaviors that allow them to manage their life, rather than their life managing them.

Now, don't hear what I am not saying. I am not saying one becomes an unemotional person who doesn't feel anything. That would be as unhealthy as just racing in with emotions out of control. I am talking about a person being strong enough to face *what is* actually happening in their life. I am talking about establishing a balance between one's mind and emotions. The reality is either one's mind or emotions is controlling the pace and direction of their life. When one's emotions are in control, their imagination is weakened and therefore the pathway to resolution and the pace to get there without confusion isn't present.

Pace is about one's imagination being stronger than their emotions. It is about one's clarity being stronger than their confusion. Sometimes it is challenging to believe one can ever control their life, but pace is critical to a person being able to connect their mind and emotions to a common agenda. When they are working together, a person has a sense of balance that will allow them the confidence to move forward with behaviors designed to strengthen their focus.

Let's go back to Cindy. I hadn't talked to her in several months. She had told me, "Talking to you is too tough. I know what you are saying is correct. I have to get my life under control, but I can't see that happening right now. I know it will either get right, or I will be dead and not have to worry about it. Just give me some time to work through all this."

With that she walked out of my life and I didn't hear from her. I would call to the check on her, but she didn't return my calls. Recently, she did call and I could hear in her voice that her life was still upside down.

Her opening words to me were, "Hey, did you think I was dead?"

"No; I knew you weren't dead."

"How did you know that? Have you been checking up on me?"

"No; I haven't been checking on you, but people have told me you were still alive and still struggling as much as ever. Is that true?"

"Which part? That I am still alive or that I am still struggling?"

"The struggling; are things any better in your life?"

"I could try to lie to you, but you would see right through it. No, things aren't any better. Richard, I am ready to just let go and let everything just fall apart. I can't take this anymore. I don't eat or sleep. The kids are feeling my pressure and reacting to it. They aren't sleeping and walk around with a cloud of sadness hanging over them. I just want this life to be over. Death seems like the best option."

"What would death solve? Yes, your life would be over, but what do you think that would do to the kids? Do you think about them in all this?"

"Of course I do! They would have to live with their father. I know what you are going to say, so save your words. You feel if they live with him, they will be destroyed through his negative presence in their life."

"You know I believe he uses them to get to you. That is going to happen as long as you allow him to have that level of control. You said some time ago that you would confront him when you felt the time was right. Are you going to do it before he kills you?"

"Richard, it won't do any good. I have tried to have that conversation with him and he either loses it or just walks away. I can't win. I just can't win."

"Cindy, there are two things you have to do. The first is to get help for the depression you are sinking deeper into.

You won't be able to see the pathway that is there for you until you can control your depression. I know your health makes it challenging for you to take prescriptions, but there has to be something you can take that won't take you down."

"I have been taking sleeping pills to help me sleep, but I have stopped. I have had these funny feelings and I know they are due to the pills. You said there were two things. What's the other one?"

"You have to move! You live too close to him. He can come and go as he pleases and uses the closeness to keep you under his control. When are you going to realize what he is doing to you, face it and stop letting him steal your spirit, use the kids and keep all of you in his prison? You can't continue to live at this pace. Physically and emotionally you don't have the energy to continue."

"I know you are right, but I can't slow my emotions down. My world just seems to be spinning faster and faster. I am totally out of control."

Is Cindy out of control? Yes! Are the emotions she is wrestling with keeping her from seeing the pathway to her finding freedom? Yes! Is there hope for her? Yes, but she is going to have to reach for it. As fast as she is moving, she can't see anything but the problems that have formed an emotional wall around her. Can she do this on her own? No! She has sunk so deep into her world of depression she can't see her way out. As long as she is moving at this emotional pace, there is no way for her to see the exit door.

This is the challenge for most people. They get caught up in their world that is spinning out of control. The faster it moves the more challenging it becomes for them to believe there is anyway out. Let their world spin fast enough and it will kill them. Stay in that spinning environment long enough and it will cause one to believe this is all there is to life.

Pace is such an important part of personal growth. If one can't manage the pace of their life, the pace of their life will manage them. The more the pace takes over the more emotional discord they will have. Pace must be controlled by one's imagination focusing on the resolution, not the problem. One's imagination allows them to have a growth plan. The challenge is the faster one is spinning emotionally, the less likely they are able to see the plan. One's imagination is sending a message that says, "Hey, here is what we need to be doing. Let's do it." Their emotions are sending an opposite message that is saying, "Hey, here is what you can't do. Stop all this foolish chatter. This is your life."

One of the two messages will be accepted and behaviors implemented to make them happen. The growth is in slowing down and trusting the mind's ability to show the pathway to resolution. That is easier to write than for most to achieve. The reason being when one is spinning out of control, they tend to not listen to healthy people. They tend to turn toward those who are just like them. There seems to be a connection based on misery. They need to exit that street and find those who are there waiting to reach out and help them. These healthy people will help them slow their life down and face what is actually happening, rather than the emotionally dysfunctional picture they keep replaying and repeating. They can do it, but not without emotionally slowing down and finding the plan that will take them toward a life of growth and improvement.

## PRINCIPLES FOR SLOWING YOUR LIFE DOWN

1. Face your life with personal honesty

2. Don't run from your fears; confront them head on.

3. Refuse to stay trapped in your circle of sameness.

4. When you can't do it on your own, don't be afraid to ask for help from the right person.

5. Find alone time and there rest in the sounds of silence.

6. Resist the temptation to run away.

7. Seek to do one positive thing for yourself each day.

8. Don't hangout with unhealthy people.

9. Keep a journal of the good things that happen each day.

10. Don't lose sight of the fact God wants you to have a healthy, productive and fulfilling life.

Chapter 13

# I'm Not Going Back There!

## Step Eight:  Refusing To Go Backward

*As long as you are looking over your shoulder for answers, you are missing the lessons that are right beside you.*

The final step in the process of one's mind and emotions working together is them *refusing to go backward.* We've heard the saying, "One step forward, two steps back?" This is how too many people live. They have this desire to challenge their life and see what they can really achieve, yet at the same time they have this fear that keeps sending them negative messages that create major internal battles. As much as they desire to move forward, for most the negative message overrides their desire.

When their desire is strong, they are willing to step out and test the waters. The challenge is what they call testing is really them sticking their toe into a pool filled with personal fear.

I spoke for the San Antonio Real Estate Investors about *The Truth About Success.* The program was based on the thought:

> *Most people don't succeed, not because they can't, but because they aren't willing to gather the knowledge and implement the behaviors necessary to move beyond their circle of sameness and reach for their dream.*

I was packing my equipment when I looked up and saw this young man standing there looking at me. I paused, noticed his name badge and said, "Gilbert, how are you doing?"

He smiled and said, "I was better before I listened to you tonight. Man, did you nail me. I am the person you were talking about. I am in this wrestling match with myself and I seem to keep getting pinned. I know what I want; I even believe I know how to get there, BUT I keep destroying what I start. I get something started and then, do what I know I shouldn't do and destroy everything. I am so tired of living this way."

There was this long pause as he stared off into space. I knew he was composing himself. This was not an easy conversation for him. He was dealing with personal accountability for his behaviors. I figured he had had this conversation several times within himself, but not with someone else.

He looked back at me with a deep sense of pain in his eyes and continued, "I mean it! I am so tired of living this way. I am so tired of lying to myself and to others. Oh, I talk a good story, but it is all a lie. When you said *Behavior Never Lies* you drove a dagger right through my heart. I wanted to get up and leave. I knew you meant that for me. I am tired of starting and then going backwards. I don't want to live this way anymore."

"Gilbert, you don't have to live that way. It is a matter of choice. Remember what I said in the beginning. Each day you get up and you make one of two choices for your life and they are the only two choices you have. You either feed your confusion or you strengthen your clarity. Whichever you choose, you implement behaviors to make that happen. Your situation is not something that just happens; it is something you design and then live out. If you don't want to live that way, you don't have to anymore. If you are tired of your circle of sameness you have the power to correct that. You have a choice and you will make it. If you are really tired of this self defeating circle you are living, the next time you feel it attacking you, you will stop and tell the Old You, *I am tired of giving into you. I am not going to do this anymore. I am going to have my dream and you are not going to stop me.*"

There are a lot of Gilbert's out there that each day fight

an inner war where one part of their life wants to jump in and go for it, but then there is that stronger presence that has had control for so long, they can't seem to get beyond the control it has over them.

I answered my phone and there was this voice on the other end shouting, "I hate my life. I hate everything about it; I hate me; I hate my job; I just hate my life."

I recognized the voice and knew it was Mindy. "Okay, what has happened to send you over this ledge?"

"Richard, I try so hard to do the things I know I need to do to get out of this rut I have been living in. I plan, I pray, I ask questions, I even listen, BUT nothing seems to help. I am just going in circles and I am tired of it. I feel like I am going backwards and I can't stop it."

How many times have people felt like Gilbert or Mindy? They push self to move forward, but only find self sliding backward and nothing they seem to do will stop it. They know what they should be doing, but just can't do it. They understand what it will take to get beyond their stumbling blocks, but each time they step forward, they get knocked backward.

The result is a collision between their imagination, which wants to get out of this pit and leap toward their dream sketch and their emotions, which want things to stay the same. This is more than a skirmish; this is an all out war for control of one's life. It is a battle between their desire to growth and all their fears about what that growth will mean. Which wins most of those skirmishes? We know the answer.

How many times has a person told self what they were going to do and then, find self still struggling with the same situation? How many times has a person been angry with

SELF because they can't seem to keep the momentum going? Oh, it is easy to start, but challenging to keep self moving in a forward direction. Why is it so challenging to stay the course? There are four common reasons I have found through working with people as their Life Coach.

First, *their behavior never really changes*. There is a big difference between changing for a moment and improving for the journey. Many people get caught up in the moment as they are forced to face the reality of their life, but the moment is just a moment where they can't sustain the energy necessary to turn their excitement into enthusiasm.

Peter put it this way. "Richard, when you are around me, it is so easy to see what I need to do. I get so pumped I am ready to change the world, BUT when you are not standing there in front of me, I lose the energy and confusion seems to come back even stronger. I am not sure I can do this on my own. It isn't that I don't want to. I just can't seem to shake these behaviors that have been a part of me for years."

This is the challenge I have faced with a few who have wanted to improve without having to change anything. When I am there, they are up, BUT because they are creating a moment and not a journey, they find it challenging to maintain the focus necessary to sustain the clarity. When we are together we talk about what they need to do to strengthen their clarity and not feed their confusion. Those are very positive conversations and they understand, BUT alone within their self they are challenged with making it happen.

What it tells me is that they have never really faced their behavior; I have faced it for them, but they haven't faced it on their own. Until they can and are willing do that, they will continue to slip back into who they have been, rather than step forward with clarity and a dedication to becoming whom they can be. They slip backward because their behavior has never really changed.

This creates an interesting challenge for those we care about and want as a part of our life. The stumbling block we have with them is their behavior. We have confronted it; they have said they were sorry and would change; we accept what they tell us even though we are skeptical; they take our forgiveness and throw it back in our face by repeating the behavior they said they were sorry for and wouldn't do again.

It is my belief that forgiveness should be earned, not just handed out. Forgiveness should be the reward for improved behavior, not words that are spoken out of a moment of guilt. As long as forgiveness is simply based on a moment, it means nothing; when it becomes the reward for improvement, it carries meaning.

The second reason many fall backward is *adjustments aren't made in a timely fashion.* Timing is such an important aspect of growth. When timing is off, the opportunity can be missed.

People have no idea how many times I have heard, "I knew it; I just knew it. I knew I was making a wrong decision, but I just couldn't seem to stop myself. I told myself not to do it, but do you know what I did? I went ahead and did it and look how it has messed up my life."

We are all emotional creatures; we have a strong sense of emotional presence and our greatest wrestling match is when we are in that battle between what our mind is telling us and what our emotions are throwing at us. As I have said before, it is more than just a moment of conflict; it is a war between one's feelings and their understanding. One is going to win and the winner gets control of their life. The next step is the implementation of behaviors designed to achieve the chosen agenda.

Susan was an emotional wreck when she arrived at my office. I had seen her upset, but never like this. As she walked into my office, she was already talking as the tears were flowing.

"Richard, I don't understand me. I am an intelligent person. I am smart and yet I let my mother tear me apart. She knows how to get to me; it is as if she has this emotional checklist and she just starts down it until she gets to the one that works that day. I tell myself I am not going to let her do this to me, but it happens time and time again. I am so angry with me right now. I want her out of my life. I don't ever want to see her again. Is that bad of me to think that way?"

"Susan, first of all she does know how to get to you. Second, she does have an emotional checklist she uses against you and third, she is only doing to your life what you are allowing her to do. When you no longer want this to happen, you will take the steps to stop it."

"I don't want her to do this to me. I don't understand how you can say that I do."

"It is easy. Your behavior says it. If you didn't want her to do this to you, you would stop her when she starts. You wouldn't give her permission to continue with the emotional beating she is putting you through. You would challenge her behavior and tell her that her behavior was no longer acceptable for your life."

"I know what you are saying, but there is this guilt factor. After all she is my mother. Doesn't the Bible teach us to respect our parents?"

"Yes! The Bible tells us to respect our parents, but I believe respect has to be a two-way street. To respect them, they must also respect you. What she is doing is disrespectful to you and that is not right. Susan, she will always be your biological mother, but when she becomes your emotional enemy, she must have to face the consequences of her behavior. If there are no consequences, there is only validation. Until you can stand up to her and challenge her behavior, she will continue. Don't you get it? Look at yourself. You are an emotional wreck because of what she has done to you. You don't respond; you let her tear you apart and then you react. You have to stop her when she is attacking. That is the time to stand up to her, not after she has waged the war and you have once again surrendered to her as her emotional prisoner. Do you understand that?"

Susan is like so many. They know what they need to do, but miss the timing of the situation. They don't grasp the fact *you can only control your emotions when they are being felt as a concern.* If one doesn't stop and address the situation while it is a concern, it will gather emotional strength and become a problem. Most problems don't get resolved; they just get continued. Then, each time a person comes face-to-face with the situation the emotions just grow. As these emotions escalate, less and less of the person wants to deal with them. What is the result? There is avoidance; one runs away; they lie and say everything is okay; they procrastinate; they allow those emotions to create a negative file that keeps getting reopened. Each time the file is opened, they go backwards and find their internal war increasing. The greater the war the more negative the emotions become. Oh, they will talk about wanting to get beyond this situation; they will tell others how much they hate the way they are feeling, but the truth is if they really hated it as much as they say, they would do something about it. Remember, *behavior never lies*.

The third reason many go backward is *confusion increases*. Follow the thought process here. One talks about wanting to get beyond their stumbling block; words are spoken, but the behaviors needed to achieve the spoken words aren't implemented. There are chances to face and move forward, but because of the emotional entanglements, they talk self out of doing anything. The common statement I hear is either, "Richard, I am going to deal with this when the timing is right" or "Richard, you don't understand. I haven't had the right moment to deal with this." Both of these are excuses. If one waits for the right moment to deal with a highly emotional situation, it won't happen in a healthy way. The longer a person procrastinates facing the issue, the more emotions get tangled up in their feelings. The stronger those feelings the easier it becomes to avoid them.

Now, put all this together and there is a picture of one confused person. Confusion is a stifling emotion. It travels with three emotional comrades that have the ability to totally paralyze a person.

There is worry; the more a person worries the more they increase their emotional entanglements.

There is doubt; the more a person doubts the more difficult it is for them to make a decision.

Then, there is uncertainty. This is where a person can really get stuck. The worry and doubt leaves them feeling they don't know what to do. They have fallen into this emotional maze and feel totally lost. Everything they look at, everything they think they should do gets caught up in this emotional funnel and they find self falling deeper and deeper into a hole they can't seem to climb out of.

Have you been there? Have you felt lost and uncertain about what to do?

How many times have we just given up in our own way? Because a person can't see a way out, they just allow this to control their life. That means one continues to implement behaviors to keep them there. Oh, they may take some steps forward, but they don't last. As soon as the confusion becomes the driving force, they go right back to that emotional sinkhole.

The last reason many keep going backward is they *keep reaching out to the wrong people*. Most people when they are lost, confused or really uncertain, they will reach out to someone and many times that someone is not the right person.

Many have told me, "Oh, I just keep everything to myself. I don't talk to anyone about what is going on inside me."

Yea, right! No one keeps the lid on when they are lost, confused or really uncertain. They might be able to do that for a short while, BUT at some point someone is going to look at them and ask, "What is wrong with you? You look terrible." That is all it takes. The emotional lid comes off and they will pour out what they are struggling with. The challenge is a person can't open that emotional pot without the other person feeling like they need to give them advice. Granted, they may not know what they are talking about, but they feel obligated to try to help them. The truth is the majority of the time they are not helping the person; they are hurting them.

How many times have we heard, "I know exactly what you are going through? I have been through that."

There it is! A shoulder of understanding; a person

who has walked the same journey and felt the same feelings understands what the person is experiencing. What do most do? They reach out to this person and they become their emotional buddy.

Here is the challenge; they don't stop and ask the right question. "Hey, have you gotten beyond it in your life? What did you learn? How did you handle all the emotional traps that you felt?"

If they can't share a healthy journey or what they did to move their life forward, DON'T LISTEN TO THEM! They can't help if they are still rehashing the yesterdays of their life. They can't offer a person healthy information if they haven't completed their own journey. If a person doesn't bring resolution, they will pull them down into their emotional sinkhole. Now both of them can throw a pity party and emotionally console each other in a very sick way.

Again, one of the most common questions I get asked by people who are struggling with improving their life is, "How do you know who to listen to and who to not listen to? It seems everyone wants to help you."

The answer to the question is simple. The wrong people will help one justify what they know they are doing wrong. They will tell them they are there for them, but in reality they just want the person to stay trapped in their Circle of Sameness. They want them there for them! They are not really there for the person. They want to use their situation to keep them at the same place they are in their moment of sameness.

The right people will really be there to bring support, BUT not by consoling the person when they are wrong. They will challenge and confront what is wrong. The genuine concern will come through in their caring behavior.

The wrong people will feed another person confusion; the right people will point them toward clarity. The wrong people will strengthen doubt; the right people will ask questions to help one face what they think they are feeling. The wrong people will become part of a person's worry; the right people will show them the pathway beyond their worry.

As long as a person is reaching out to the wrong people, they will be going backward. As long as they are listening to people who only speak through their opinions, they are relying on people who can only show them the pathway backward, not forward.

Don't forget! The people who aren't growing can only show someone how to stay where they are. People who are reliving their yesterday can't point another toward a tomorrow filled with improvement.

## PRINCIPLES FOR STANDING FIRM

1. Don't listen to those who don't know what they are talking about.

2. Create a foundation of beliefs and stand firm on them.

3. Refuse to get sucked into another's negative agenda.

4. Don't let the "Old You" set the agenda for your life.

5. Challenge your mind each day.

6. Don't let your emotions be your guiding force.

7. Remember that the Circle of Sameness is a trap that halts growth.

8. Don't forget that yesterday is a reference library, not a room to live in.

9. Protect yourself from people who want to control you.

10. Remember, all behavior has an agenda.

Chapter 14

# Behavior Really Doesn't Lie

## Conclusion

*The essence of any person is not what they say but what they do.*

Is the picture clear? Living in sync is about a person's mind and emotions sharing a common agenda. If one's emotions has one agenda and their imagination another, they are going to live a confused life. They will demonstrate that fact each day through their behavior.

This is why I keep repeating those three little words, *Behavior Never Lies*. The essence of who any person is, is not defined by what they say. It is defined by what they do. As long as they say one thing and do another, they are trapped in their own wasteland. In that wasteland they are doomed to live a life that *can't* offer them inner happiness, a sense of personal fulfillment or a definition to personal freedom. They will awaken each day uncertain about what that day means; they will end each day wondering what happened. They will walk through an existence never experiencing what they were placed on this earth to achieve.

None of us are here to live a life of misery. That is not God's intention for any person's life. Each person is here to explore their talents and find the joy that comes from translating their talents into positive behavior.

We are not on this earth to end each day questioning why we are alive. We have been placed on this earth to be fulfilled through our presence. We are here to have a presence that is present when we are not present.

We are not here to be a prisoner! We are here to be free. What does that mean? It means we are here to be an original! We are not to get up each day and walk out as an actor in someone else's play that they have written for our life. We are to be the INDIVIDUAL God intended and designed us to be. That is why the #1 thought for my life is *why spend my energy being a carbon copy when I am the original.* Our value is not in being what others want to program us to be. Our value is to find our unique gifts, develop them and create a presence that has presence when we are not present.

Our life is OURS to live. Yes, there are others who will share it with us. Yes, we will be a part of something greater than simply being an individual. Yes, we will have to blend our personality with the personalities of others, BUT none of this is about us giving up being an original. Each of us really does get to choose who we are. Will others have an influence on us? Absolutely, but that doesn't mean they get to program us. Will others help us understand who we are and what we can achieve? Absolutely, but they are there to help, not to take control of our life and make us into who they want us to be.

It is one's choice to make. If one wants to know who they think they are, study the behavior. If one wants to know what they can achieve, study their behavior. If one wants to understand what their future will be, study their behavior.

If THEY don't like the picture THEY are seeing, study the connection between what is being said and what is being acted out through behavior. Why! The answer is the still those three words – *Behavior Never Lies!*

## Share It With Others

To order copies of this book,
Call 1-800-368-8255
or (757) 873-7722
or visit
www.RichardFlint.com

Special quantity discounts are available
for bulk purchases.

Please allow 2-3 weeks for US delivery.
Canada & International orders
please allow 4-6 weeks for delivery.

Other Books by Richard Flint, CSP:

Building Blocks *For Strengthening Your Life*

Building Blocks *For Strengthening Your Relationships*

Building Blocks *For Improving Customer Relationships*

Building Blocks *For Controlling Stress*

Breaking Free

Quiet Please

Feelings

It Takes A Lot Of Pain To Grow Up

Reflections

Sometimes I Really Need To Cry